A NEW LAW FOR A NEW PEOPLE

A NEW LAW FOR A NEW PEOPLE

By
Frederick K.C. Price, Ph.D.

Faith One Publishing
Los Angeles, California

Unless otherwise indicated, all Scripture quotations are taken from the *King James Version* of the Bible.

A New Law for a New People
ISBN 1-883798-01-9
Copyright © 1993 by
Frederick K.C. Price
P.O. Box 90000
Los Angeles, CA 90009

Published by Faith One Publishing
7901 South Vermont Avenue
Los Angeles, California 90044

Contents

PROLOGUE

There are certain denominations whose doctrines are based on the Old Testament — or rather *the Law.* Unfortunately, these denominations have not made a distinction between the Abrahamic Covenant and the New Covenant founded on the blood of the Lord Jesus Christ.

God gave and established the covenant with Abraham for one primary purpose, and that purpose was to bring into existence a people who would have a special relationship — a covenant relationship — with Him. Out of this special group, the Redeemer of mankind would come.

God informed Satan in Genesis 3:15 that the *"seed of the woman"* would bruise his head, and "you [Satan] will bruise his heel." This is the first mention in the Bible of the giving and coming of a Redeemer or a Savior.

In the twelfth chapter of the Book of Genesis, God called to Abraham and told him to come out from his father's house into a land He would show him. God told Abraham that He would make of him a great nation and that He would establish His covenant with him (Gen. 17:4). Out of the loins of Abraham came a nation that had never been on the face of the earth before, and out of that nation came the Redeemer of the world.

At a certain period of time, Abraham produced a son called Isaac. Isaac produced a son called Jacob, and Jacob had twelve sons. One of these twelve sons was named Joseph. The other sons became envious and jealous of their brother Joseph, and sold him into slavery in Egypt. God was with Joseph and showed him favor. Eventually, Joseph was elevated to become the second-highest ranking person in the nation of Egypt.

The ruler of Egypt, Pharaoh, had a dream which bothered him. God gave Joseph the interpretation of that dream, which Joseph explained to Pharaoh. He informed the ruler that there would be seven years of plenty, followed by seven years of famine. The king wanted to know what they should do to prepare for this calamity. God gave Joseph the wisdom to know what to do, and he informed the king. Egypt collected all of the food and rationed it out during the seven plenteous years so that they would have enough during the lean years.

The end result was that because of Joseph's success in Egypt, Jacob, his sons, and their descendants came to Egypt to live. Pharaoh welcomed Joseph's family, and gave them a place of residence in the suburbs — a land called Goshen.

As time went on, the children of Israel (the name given to Jacob by the Lord) prospered and multiplied in the land of Egypt. Eventually Joseph died, then Jacob died and so did all of his sons. A new king came on the throne in Egypt who did not know Joseph, and he was not kindly disposed to the children of Israel because of their numbers and prosperity. He enslaved them and took away all of the privileges they once

2

enjoyed during the time of the old Pharaoh. The Israelites cried out to God, and after some 400 years had passed, God sent a man named Moses to deliver them.

When Moses and the children of Israel left Egypt, they left a mighty nation. Moses led them out of captivity across the Red Sea and on towards "a land flowing with milk and honey" called *the Promised Land*.

At that time, all they had was the memory of a covenant and the seal of that covenant which was circumcision. They had no law, they had no priesthood and they had no religious or spiritual teaching. They came to Mount Sinai, and through Moses, God gave them the Law of the Covenant. The Law is that which allows the covenant to be manifested. The covenant is what God established. The Law is what the Israelites had to do so that God would be free to bring to pass in their lives the benefits of the covenant He had established with them.

He gave them the priesthood, the sacrifices, the offerings and the interpretation of the Law — all the things God expected Israel to observe and to perform. *The priesthood and everything associated with it were given to the Israelites ONLY!* The Gentiles were never given these laws, nor did the Gentiles ever have any part in the benefits of the Law. As long as the children of Israel kept the Law of the Covenant unbroken and unviolated, it is an historical fact that there was no sickness or disease among the whole nation, nor could any nation stand against them and overcome them in combat or warfare. When the Israelites violated the Law, however, they got into serious trouble.

Israel began to digress from God and they wandered into selfishness, greed and idolatry. As a result, they opened the door for a heathen nation called Babylon, under a king called Nebuchadnezzar to overcome them. This heathen nation came to Jerusalem, the seat of the nation of Israel, desecrated the Temple, took away the golden vessels and everything that was in the Temple and carried off the children of Israel as captives into the country of Babylon. The Israelites were faced day and night with extreme heathenism, but Almighty God intervened while they were in captivity, and set them free from idolatrous worship.

God used several men to keep the Law alive among the Israelites during their Babylonian captivity. Among them was a man named Daniel. He interpreted the king's dream and a mysterious handwriting on a wall, and was miraculously delivered from the lions' den, unscathed and unscratched. These events so shook the heathen nation that King Nebuchadnezzar declared that Daniel's God was the true and living God and He alone was to be worshiped.

Then there were the three Hebrew boys — Shadrach, Meshach and Abednego. They were given the opportunity to worship the golden image the king had erected. Because they refused to worship the image, the king had them thrown into a fiery furnace which he had heated up seven times hotter than normal. When he looked inside the furnace, instead of seeing three persons, he saw four people walking around. This so shook the king that he declared that the God of the three Hebrews boys was the God who was to be worshiped.

Eventually the children of Israel were set free from their Babylonian captivity. But from the time of Daniel until the time of Christ, the Israelites became very sectarian in their thinking and gradually moved away from the dictates of the true Law. They did not get into idol worship to the extent that they could have if they had remained in Babylon, but they got away from the Law. They started adding a lot of their traditions to it. By the time Jesus came on the scene, there were several different beliefs in circulation regarding the "supposed" Law, represented by several different groups — the Sadducees, the Pharisees and the Scribes. By this time, the Law had become so messed up and botched up that it did not look anything like what God had originally given Moses.

The Law was not given to the Gentile nations, but only to God's covenant people — the sons of Abraham. Jesus actually interpreted the Law the way it should have been interpreted. He called Israel back to the covenant and challenged them to leave their traditions and the doctrines of men and to fulfill the covenant God had made with Abraham and to operate in the Law of that Covenant. It is interesting to note that in all of the four gospels, there is no indication that Jesus ever required or expected any of the Gentile world to keep the Law.

Do not think that Gentile believers are foot-loose and fancy free, and that they do not have things they are supposed to have. We have a law under the New Covenant as well. We have responsibilities as Christians, but we need to keep things in their right places like they are supposed to be kept and not intermingle them or try to mix oil with water because that will not work.

THE NEW COVENANT vs. THE OLD

In the second chapter of Ephesians, we see a tremendous revelation concerning God's relationship to those who are considered Gentiles.

> **Wherefore remember, that ye being in time past Gentiles....**
>
> **(Eph. 2:11)**

The implication here is that the people to whom Paul was writing were not considered as Gentiles when he was writing to them. No, they were the Church — the Body of Christ — at Ephesus. Originally they were Gentiles; however, when they accepted Christ as their Savior and embraced the Gospel of the Lord Jesus, they left the realm of the Gentiles, as far as God was concerned, and entered into a third group known as the Church.

As far as God is concerned, there are only three ethnic groups of people on the face of planet earth today. Anthropologists have divided mankind into many different groups, but God recognizes only three classes of men and women on this planet — one is the Jew, the second is the Gentile and the third is the Body of Christ. Everyone who is not a Jew is a Gentile, and believers in Christ form the Body of Christ. The Body of Christ is made up of both Jews and Gentiles. Once a person accepts Christ as his or her personal Savior, he or she moves out of the realm of being a Jew or a Gentile, from a spiritual standpoint, and he or she moves into the realm of being a member of the Body of Christ.

Paul is writing to a group of people who apparently were formerly Gentiles because he reminds them of their former status:

> **Wherefore remember, that ye being in time past Gentiles in the flesh, who are called Uncircumcision by that which is called the Circumcision in the flesh made by hands.**
>
> **(Eph. 2:11)**

When God established the covenant with Abraham, He gave him a sign or a seal of that covenant, which was circumcision. The males under that covenant were to have the foreskins of their penises removed after they were eight days old — *that was the sign of the covenant, and it was a sign in the flesh.* That seal would always be there. There was no way one could get rid of it. It was a sign for all times.

During the time of Paul, those of Jewish ancestry were called either Jews, Israelites, Hebrews or sometimes they were referred to as the circumcision because of their Abrahamic Covenant, and the seal of that covenant which was circumcision.

> **That at that time ye were without Christ, being aliens from the commonwealth of Israel, and strangers from the covenants of promise, having no hope, and without God in the world.**
>
> **(Eph. 2:12)**

If you are without hope and without God in the world, *then you have to also be without the covenant of God* and without the blessing of God, and, therefore, it would not do you any good to follow the dictates of the covenant.

AN ALIEN IS A FOREIGNER.

One who is a foreigner or an alien is one who does not have the legal rights which are guaranteed to those who are legal citizens of a particular country or nation. When a person is a foreigner, he is outside the benefits of the country he is residing in — he is an alien. This is what verse twelve is saying about the Gentile world. This is talking about every non-Jew before he or she accepted Christ as Savior.

Now if you are a stranger from the covenant, how are you supposed to keep the Law of the Covenant?

For example, when you go to a foreign country, you are there by grace. You may have a visa or a passport, but you are just a visitor. The officials could boot you out as quickly as they wanted to — you are not a citizen — you have no rights! In other words, you are a stranger from the covenant of citizenship. *This is the same thing Paul is talking about. He said that as Gentiles, we are aliens, strangers from the covenant of promise that God made to the Jews.* Therefore, how could you possibly be under the Law of the Covenant when you are a stranger to the covenant.

> "...having no hope, and without God in the world."
>
> **(Eph. 2:12)**

If you are without God, you have to be without the Law of God. If you do not have God, how are you

8

going to have His law? How could you be required to keep His law?

No one was under the Law in the days of Christ, but the Jews. What did Jesus come to the earth for? Most everyone thinks Jesus came to die at Calvary, but that is actually a residual benefit of His coming.

JESUS CAME TO FULFILL THE COVENANT! All that God had promised Abraham, and all the things God had promised would come to pass were going to come to pass through the Messiah. Jesus came to fulfill the covenant. Since this is the case, this should tell us then that *when the covenant was fulfilled, THE COVENANT WOULD STOP FUNCTIONING.* When the covenant stopped functioning, it means it is no longer in force because it is no longer needed. How then can someone 2,000 years later be required to keep the Law of a covenant that is not even in force?

THE COVENANT WAS FULFILLED

Consequently, the Law of the Covenant stopped functioning. The priesthood ceased to minister before Jehovah, and the sacrifices no longer had any meaning whatsoever. They had been fulfilled. We do not need them anymore. When Jesus came to fulfill the Old Covenant, He established a New Covenant with a new priesthood and with a brand-new group of people.

The first people who were covenant people were born of circumcised parentage. Abraham was circumcised as the sign of the covenant God had established with him. That means when he and his wife had a child, that child came as a result of circumcised parentage.

The second people who were covenant people were "born of the Spirit," and instead of circumcision of the flesh, they have circumcision of the spirit — that is circumcision of the heart in the inner man.

The circumcision of this new group of people is known as *THE NEW BIRTH.*

> **For he is not a Jew, which is one outwardly; neither is that circumcision, which is outward in the flesh: But he is a Jew, which is one inwardly; and circumcision is that of the heart, in the spirit, and not in the letter; whose praise is not of men, but of God.**
> **(Rom. 2:28-29)**

THE CHURCH IS SPIRITUAL ISRAEL

The Jewish people who are in the world today have a heritage that goes back to the covenant God established with Abraham. Even though at this present time the Old Covenant has been set aside, God still remembers that special, covenant-relationship He had with Abraham and, subsequently, with Abraham's descendents. The Body of Christ is spiritual Israel. *There is physical Israel, and there is SPIRITUAL ISRAEL.* We, as Christians, are spiritual Israel, because we, too, have a special, covenant-relationship with the heavenly Father; therefore, we can say we are "spiritual Jews."

You cannot have circumcision of the heart until you are born again, and you cannot be born again until you accept Jesus Christ as your personal Lord and Savior. When you become born again, you change from the "old man of sin" into a "new man in Christ Jesus." However, this time instead of the seal of the covenant with God being an outward physical sign, the circumcision of the flesh, it is a spiritual sign, the circumcision of the heart.

A NEW LAW FOR A NEW PEOPLE

With this new-creation people came the New Law. If we have a new covenant, we have to have a new law. There was the Old Covenant God had established, and with that covenant was the Law. The Ten Commandments formed a part of that Law. If we have a New Covenant, then that ought to tell us that the Old Covenant must have been superseded by the New Covenant. If you have a New Covenant, that means the Old Covenant is not in operation, and if the Old Covenant is not in operation, neither is the Law of the Old Covenant, so that puts the Ten Commandments out of business!

I AM NOT OPPOSED TO THE TEN COMMANDMENTS — I do not personally have anything against the Ten Commandments. All I want to do is to show you where we, as Christians, are from the standpoint of what the Bible says, rather than from the standpoint of what theology and demoninationalism and traditionalism say, so that we can get in line with the Word of God and receive the benefits of the New Covenant.

If we have a New Covenant, then we have some benefits, and we ought to be walking in those benefits. You cannot compromise the rights of the New Covenant by trying to hang on to the Old Covenant.

Christians are struggling to keep the Ten Commandments, which is the old law of the Old Covenant, which is not even in force, and are neglecting to keep the Law of the New Covenant. It is a shame, because the Spirit of God is calling the Church back to the law of the New Covenant, just as Jesus was calling Israel back to the law of the Old Covenant when He walked the earth. He was calling them away from their traditions, calling them away from their theologies, calling them away from what they had said and what they thought and calling them back to the original law of what God had said. Christians are under a New Covenant now, and we have a law, and we need to learn how to operate in that law.

In John 13, we find the Law of the New Covenant. This is Jesus Christ himself speaking. He is the One who fulfilled the Old Covenant. He is the One who established the New Covenant, and He is the One who has outlined very clearly and definitely the Law of the New Covenant.

> **A new commandment I give unto you, That ye love one another; as I have loved you, that ye also love one another. By this shall all men know that ye are my disciples, if ye have love one to another.**
> **(John 13:34,35)**

BY THIS...

"By this" — not by casting out demons, not by laying hands on the sick, not by paying your tithes, not by going to church fifteen times a week, not by raising your hands, not by saying, "Praise the Lord," not by casting out deaf-and-dumb spirits, not by working miracles. We ought to do these things, but Jesus did not say that this is the way the world would know we are His disciples. He said we would be known by the love we show one another.

LOVE IS THE NEW LAW!

LOVE is the Law of the New Covenant. Jesus did not say, "A new *suggestion* I give unto you." He said *"COMMANDMENT."* This means you do not have any choice about it if you want to stay in God's good graces.

If you walk under the covenant and call yourself blood-bought and blood-washed, you have an obligation to keep the Law of the New Covenant, and the Law is a *LAW OF LOVE!* It does not mean running around hugging your brothers and your sisters and patting them on their backs. It means treating your brother right, it means treating your sister right — that is what it means. It means to stop running our brothers and sisters down with our tongues. It means to stop lying about people or to them, to stop being envious and jealous and strifeful. *This is what walking in love means!*

The Bible says that love works no ill towards one's neighbor (or brother or sister) (Rom. 13:10). This is why God does not have to give you a "thou shalt not steal" and a "thou shalt not lie" and a "thou shalt not do this, that, or the other." If you love me, you will not lie to me or about me. If you love me, you will not steal from me, and if you love me, you will not try to go to bed with my wife. Jesus said the world will know that we are His disciples because we are concerned about each other, we treat each other right, we do not talk about each other, we do not run one another down, we do not bear false witness against our brethren, we are not committing fornication and adultery with our brothers and sisters in Christ.

Notice, Jesus did not say, "A new commandment I give unto you, that you love the world." He said that by your love for one another, the world will recognize you as a disciple. "I have never seen this kind of love before." That is what the world's reaction will be when that kind of love is demonstrated!

THAT IS THE LAW OF THE NEW COVENANT

And Jesus said *it is a commandment!* You have a commandment to love me. You may not like me, but you have to love me, and I may not like you, but I have to love you.

Under the Old Covenant, they had a high priest. Under the New Covenant, we also have a High Priest. *JESUS CHRIST, THE LORD OF GLORY, IS OUR HIGH PRIEST.*

> **Now of the things which we have spoken this is the sum: we have such an high priest, who is set on the right hand of the throne of the Majesty in the heavens; A minister of the sanctuary, and of the true tabernacle, which the Lord pitched, and not man.**
> **(Heb. 8:1-2)**

Notice what it says here: "We have such an high priest...." Jesus is our High Priest. We have a covenant, we have a law and we have a High Priest.

When the Old Covenant was in operation, there was a law, a priesthood and a physical place of worship — the Temple. The Temple was divided into three compartments. The original portable tabernacle that

14

was built under Moses was designed according to this plan, and when Solomon built a permanent temple for Jehovah God, it was built after the pattern of the tabernacle.

In the three sections of the Temple there was the outer court, the holy place and the Holy of Holies or the Most Holy Place. Only the high priest could go into the Holy of Holies once a year. The reason God made the Temple the way He did was because He wanted the Temple's design to correspond with or to represent the threefold nature of man.

Inside the Holy of Holies was what was called the Mercy Seat. On either side of the Mercy Seat were two angels with their wings outstretched, overshadowing and protecting the Mercy Seat. Once a year, God Almighty would come down in His Shekinah glory, and He would reside at the Mercy Seat. The high priest would come and he would go into the Holy of Holies and minister to God on behalf of the people.

THE THREEFOLD NATURE OF MAN

The body and flesh of man correspond to the outer court. The holy place corresponds to the soul of man, and the Holy of Holies or Most Holy Place correspond to man's spirit. God is not to be met in the outer court. God is not met in the holy place, but God resides on the Mercy Seat in the inner man, in the Holy of Holies — THE SPIRIT OF MAN.

Sometimes Christians get caught up in what they hear preachers say, and they do not really read the Bible for themselves. I was guilty of this at one time. In fact, I would wind my sermon up and bring it to a "hallelujah" conclusion concerning Jesus hanging on the cross, and the fact that when He was about to give up the ghost, He cried, "IT IS FINISHED" (John 19:30). I would say, "Praise God, when Jesus said 'It is finished,' that meant salvation was bought and paid for. It was wrapped up, signed, sealed and delivered."

THAT IS NOT TRUE!

SALVATION WAS NOT FINISHED! Jesus had not even died yet. When He made that statement, He was still alive. Men were still under bondage; they were still in sin. No, He was not talking about salvation being finished. In fact, salvation had not even started yet because it would not start until Jesus went into hell, and it would not be over until He rose from the dead.

Well, what did Jesus mean when He said, "It is finished"? He meant that the *ABRAHAMIC COVENANT WAS FINISHED!* He meant the Old Testament was finished. He meant that a New Covenant was coming in.

> **Jesus, when he had cried again with a loud voice, yielded up the ghost** [or spirit]. **And, behold, the veil of the temple was rent in twain from the top to the bottom; and the earth did quake, and the rocks rent.**
> **(Matt. 27:50-51)**

There was a veil between the holy place and the Holy of Holies. Only the high priest could go back into the Holy of Holies once a year, and he had to come with blood. The sacrificial blood of the Atonement. If he did not do that, he would be struck dead instantly.

When Jesus died on the cross, He came to fulfill the Abrahamic Covenant. He said (in Matthew 5:17),

16

that He did not come to destroy the Law or the Prophets rather, He came to fulfill the Law. Jesus was known as "Shiloh," and the Bible said that "the sceptre shall not depart from Judah, nor a lawgiver from between his feet, until Shiloh come." (Gen. 49:10) *JESUS CHRIST IS SHILOH, AND HE HAS COME!*

When He said, "IT IS FINISHED," and bowed His head and yielded up the ghost (or spirit), the Bible said that a mighty angel came into the Temple, into the holy place, and grabbed the veil that was hanging from the ceiling, separating the people in the holy place from the Holy of Holies and tore it in two from the ceiling to the floor (Matt. 27:51; Mark 15:38; Luke 23:45). The way of access to God was made open. There is no more veil to keep man from God, and Jesus Christ is the High Priest who is ministering to God on our behalf. We can go directly into the throne-room of God. The Bible tells us to come boldly to the Throne of Grace to find help in time of need (Heb. 4:16).

The covenant has been fulfilled. We have access to God. When that veil was torn in two that meant that the sacrifices stopped, it meant that the high priest's office stopped, it meant that the covenant and the Law were finished. Jesus has established a new law, and it is the *LAW OF LOVE*.

The following chapters explore in depth, with supporting Scriptures, the issues concerning *THE CHURCH* and *THE MOSAIC LAW*.

1

THE CHURCH AND THE TEN COMMANDMENTS

If you have been a Christian for any length of time, you have probably been confronted with the idea at some time or another that you, as a Christian, are to keep the Ten Commandments. And, of course, it sounds very reasonable that Christians would keep the commandments contained in the Law of Moses, historically known as the Mosaic Law or simply as the Law. However, I believe that this concept needs to be clarified because there has been much confusion and some misconception in the Body of Christ concerning the Law, more specifically, "The Ten Commandments." First, I want to ask the following question and then deal with the subject at length: *IS THE CHURCH UNDER THE MOSAIC LAW?*

There are certain denominations which have doctrines based on the Old Testament and on keeping the Law. There are certain Pentecostal and holiness groups that say you have to keep the Ten Commandments. In fact, they say you are not saved if you don't. Consequently, I believe it needs to be clearly defined and delineated if in fact Christians are required by the Word to keep the Ten Commandments and to observe the Law.

In my estimation, the denominational church world has never made a clear distinction between the Abrahamic Covenant and the New Covenant established in the blood of the Lord Jesus Christ. When the New Covenant was ushered in, there was a New Law of the covenant, there was a new people and there was a new priesthood.

The Levitical priesthood was over. Jesus Christ is the High Priest of the new priesthood. The High Priest is the main priest, the top priest. However, there are other priests under Him, and we are a part of that group and we need to know who we are.

> **Wherefore laying aside all malice, and all guile,**
> **and hypocrisies, and envies, and all evil speakings.**
> **(1 Pet. 2:1)**

This Scripture really is not a part of the main topic of this book. However, it is of such significance for us as Christians to be on the right track with God that I feel duty bound to make a comment here regarding this Scripture. So that when we get further into our study, we will be able to understand how the Word of God applies to us in this area.

There are many Christians who have malice in their hearts. It does not mean they are not saved or that they do not love God, but they are harboring malice in their spirits — malice against their husbands, against their wives, against their brothers and sisters in the Body of Christ, against their pastors, or others and this should not be.

Peter did not say we are to pray it away, because you cannot pray malice away — and you cannot fast it away. He says to lay it aside. That means, then, the responsibility is mine and it is yours. We have to volitionally do this by an act of our wills. ''LAY ASIDE ALL...'' You cannot hold onto even a little bit of it. There are some Christians who attempt to hold onto a ''little'' malice — they are willing to give up 95%, but they try and hold unto the 5%. No, we have to *lay all of it aside: ALL MALICE, ALL GUILE, ALL HYPOCRISIES, ALL ENVIES AND ALL EVIL SPEAKING!*

There is a lot of hypocrisy in the Body of Christ, and it needs to be revealed for what it is. Some Christians go to church and sing to the Lord with raised hands and a holy look on their faces, but they are living hypocritical lives. They may be living with someone as their husband or wife when, in fact, they are not married or they are not even on speaking terms with their husbands or wives.

It is pitiful to see Christians envying one another. There is nothing for them to be envious about. If they feel God is blessing someone more than themselves, they should find out why. There has to be a reason for it. They should find out why and then bring their lives in line with the truth so they can get blessed too. Do not be envious of anyone. Be glad the person is being blessed — be glad that people are experiencing the blessings of God. That lets you know God is still in the blessing business. And as long as He is, there is an opportunity for you to reap the blessings He has in store for all His children who love and serve Him.

21

Watch your mouth. Some Christians need to learn how to put a zipper on their lips. They talk too much to the wrong people at the wrong time. Spirit-filled, faith-believing, Bible-toting believers need to be careful about whom they hold conversations with, and they need to be careful about what they talk about in those conversations. You should never, but never as a Christian talk to a non-Christian (whether it be your spouse, relative, friend or anyone else) about Kingdom business, because they are not in the Kingdom, and they cannot understand what you are talking about. Most times, all they will do is make a mockery out of what you are saying. The only thing you talk to a sinner about is his or her need to receive Christ as his or her personal Savior and his or her need to become born again. What is happening in the congregation of believers is none of the sinner's business.

Do not let evil speaking come out of your mouth, and do not let anyone tell you anything that is evil about another person. The majority of the time, it is nothing but envy and jealousy and the devil trying to stir up strife.

> **As newborn babes, desire the sincere milk of the word, that ye may grow thereby: If so be ye have tasted that the Lord is gracious. To whom coming, as unto a living stone, disallowed indeed of men, but chosen of God, and precious. Ye also, as lively stones, are built up a spiritual house, an holy priesthood...**
> **(1 Pet. 2:1-5)**

THAT IS WHO CHRISTIANS ARE!

If you are going to operate and stand in the office of a priest, you cannot do so with malice, guile, hypocrisy, envy and evil speaking coming out of your mouth. These things do not qualify you to be "an holy priesthood." That is why the Bible tells us to lay aside all these things because they are against who we are in Christ Jesus.

> ...an holy priesthood, to offer up spiritual sacrifices, acceptable to God by Jesus Christ.
>
> (1 Pet. 2:5)

Notice the words *"spiritual sacrifices."* The Law of Moses required no spiritual sacrifices, just physical ones. Denying yourself certain foods, going to church on Saturday, offering a lamb or a ram or a turtle dove for a sin offering — all these are physical and outward forms of sacrifice.

God does not want us to be sick, down, scared or going without our needs met. He receives no glory from our going without this, or going without that, or by our not eating this food or not eating that food. These are not the kind of sacrifices God wants us to perform. That is what those under the Law did. They could not eat this, they could not eat that, and they could not do this and they could not do that. *We, as children of God, are to make SPIRITUAL sacrifices.*

HOW DO WE DO THAT?

> By him [Jesus] therefore let us offer the sacrifice of praise to God continually, that is, the fruit of our lips giving thanks to his name.
>
> (Heb. 13:15)

"THE SACRIFICE OF PRAISE"

That is the sacrifice God wants our "holy priesthood" to offer! How do we do that? With our mouths, by making a joyful noise unto the Lord, speaking forth His praises, telling forth and extolling God's goodness.

> **Wherefore laying aside all malice, and all guile, and hypocrisies, and envies, and all evil speakings.**
> **(1 Pet. 2:1)**

You cannot praise the Lord and speak evil at the same time. Jesus said you cannot get sweet water and bitter water out of the same fountain. You cannot have evil speaking and praise for the Lord coming out of your mouth at the same time.

The Apostle Paul said that there is nothing unclean of itself (Rom. 14:14). He was speaking about ceremonial uncleanness in reference to the Jew. Under the Old Covenant, there were certain animals that were classified as clean and unclean. Unclean animals were never to be used in sacrifices to Jehovah God. It was not that the animals were dirty, it was just a distinction that God made between certain animals. But Paul said there is nothing unclean of itself, except to that man who thinks it is unclean. All things are made by God and they are to be received with thanksgiving. Let's go back to First Peter, and cover some other things concerning who we are in Christ Jesus.

> **Wherefore also it is contained in the scripture,**
> **Behold, I lay in Sion a chief corner stone, elect,**
> **precious: and he that believeth on him shall not be**

confounded. Unto you therefore which believe he is precious: but unto them which be disobedient, the stone which the builders disallowed, the same is made the head of the corner. And a stone of stumbling, and a rock of offence, even to them which stumble at the word, being disobedient: whereunto also they were appointed. But ye are a chosen generation, a royal priesthood, an holy nation, a peculiar people; that ye should shew forth the praises of him who hath called you out of darkness into his marvellous light.

(1 Pet. 2:6-9)

That is why we shout, that is why we clap our hands, because we have been called out of darkness into His light. Many of us, before we were born again, walked in darkness for many years. There wasn't anything to shout about in the dark. But, praise God, we are in the light now, and there is a whole lot to shout about, because we are getting to see all the things we could not see when we were in the dark.

Which in time past were not a people, but are now the people of God: which had not obtained mercy, but now have obtained mercy.

(1 Pet. 2:10)

WE ARE A ROYAL PRIESTHOOD!

There is a two-fold priesthood we are involved in under this New Covenant. First of all, we are a holy priesthood. The holy priesthood offers up spiritual sacrifices and praises. In other words, we extol and tell about the goodness of God. We praise His name, and we give Him honor and glory in verbal ways. Now the royal priesthood, on the other hand, deals with the things concerning God by His Word.

The holy priesthood function is our personal, private extolling and exalting of the Lord. We can also do that publicly, but it is primarily for our personal and private worship. In our royal priesthood function, we extol and present the things of God and the things of Christ through the Word of God — it is the manifestation that comes through the Word.

The question that confronts the Church today is, *"What is the Church's relationship to the old Covenant?"* The answer is, "IT HAS NO RELATIONSHIP — none at all! No Gentile was ever under the Old Covenant, nor could he get under it except in very rare situations. He would have to submit to circumcision and then he would have to go through a special ritual in order to be included in Judaism as a proselyte. But ordinarily, no Gentile was under the Law because the Law was not given to him. The covenant was not made with him. The covenant was made with the seed of Abraham, and with no one else. In fact, no Jew or Israelite can get into the Old Covenant today. And yet periodically we see the Jew attempting to follow the dictates of the Law. *It is a waste of time!* It may put salve on one's conscience but it does not register on Jehovah BECAUSE THE LAW HAS BEEN SET ASIDE. The Old Covenant has been fulfilled. It is not functioning or operating anymore. No one can get into the Old Covenant now or at any time in the future, because there is no longer an Old Covenant, not as far as God is concerned.

People can try to keep something going and go through the rituals of a thing, but it is empty —

it has no life simply because it is over. The Old Covenant has been done away with. A New Covenant is now in its place!

IS THE CHURCH TO KEEP THE TEN COMMANDMENTS?

My answer is: "No!" You might say I could just be arbitrarily saying no. I am not God, so we should have more than just Fred Price saying no.

Certain denominations say if you are a Christian, you had better keep the Law. They worship and go to church on Saturdays. They keep the Law of the Sabbath, and they believe that anyone who does not do so, has something wrong with them. They also keep the Ten Commandments or make an attempt to keep them.

Let us start with the premise that the Church is supposed to keep the Ten Commandments — just like Israel was supposed to keep them. If that is true, then you can easily analyze this and see it for yourself. You do not have to know anything about theology. All you have to do is just have a brain and a mind that is working normally. I am serious, you do not even have to have an education or anything, and you will be able to see this very clearly. We always reason from the known to the unknown. There is no other way you can reason. So we will start out with an intellectual premise and then we will move to a spiritual reality.

Think about this: if the Church is required by the Father God to keep the same Ten Commandments that the children of Israel were required to keep, then that would mean that the Church would have to be in the same spiritual condition the children of Israel were in when the Law was given to them. Why was the Law given to Israel in the first place? God gave the Law to them because Israel was spiritually dead. He could not appeal to them from the standpoint of the "inward man" because their "inward man" had died through Adam's sin in the Garden of Eden. The only way God could deal with any man, including Israel, was in an outward, physical, tangible, visible way. Therefore, since He could not deal with them from the "inward man," He could not fill them with His Holy Spirit, and then tap into them through the "spirit man." He had to deal with them from outward, observable manifestations. So He gave them laws that would cause them to be conscious of Him by saying, "Thou shalt, and Thou shalt not...."

Since God gave the Ten Commandments to spiritually dead men in order to govern them, are you going to tell me that now that God has made us alive in Christ and made us new creatures according to Second Corinthians 5:17 ("Therefore if any man be in Christ, he is a new creature: old [covenants] things are passed away; behold, all [covenants] things are become new") that we have to follow the same law He gave to spiritually dead men?

WE ARE BRAND-NEW IN HIM!

If we are to keep the old Law as Christians, then we are going to have to revert back to the same spiritual condition Israel was in when God gave them the covenant. They were incapable of loving one another with the *agape*-kind of love because they did not have the capacity to love this way. That is why, when Jesus

28

ushered in the New Covenant, He said in John 13: *"A new commandment I give unto you, That you love one another. . .By this shall all men know that ye are my disciples, if ye have love one to another"* (John 13:34,35).

It is not because you keep the Sabbath day, not because you refuse to eat certain kinds of food, not because you bring a turtle dove or ram or a goat as an offering for your sin. He said that the world would know you are His disciples because you have love one to another, and you cannot love one another without having the *agape*-kind (the God kind) of love.

This is because spiritually dead men have no way of appreciating love. The only thing they can do is to have some kind of emotional feeling, some kind of intellectual attachment or something like that, but they do not and cannot have *agape* love because they do not have the capacity for it. They have to have a new spirit, they have to have a new heart and the only way you can get a new heart is through the new birth. No one can tell me that if God gave a law to spiritually dead men, then He would turn around and give us a New Covenant, making us spiritually alive, and then He would require us to keep the same law that dead men kept. That does not make sense, intellectually or spiritually.

THE CHURCH IS SPIRITUALLY ALIVE!

The Body of Christ — the Church — is not supposed to keep the Ten Commandments. The Church is supposed to walk in the new Law — the Law of Love — the *agape*-kind of love, and that love is to control every action and everything we do. No, we are not required to keep the Ten Commandments. The Ten

Commandments are an attempt on the part of man to make himself worthy in the sight of God. The only thing that can make you worthy is the *blood of Jesus Christ!*

The Bible says, "For by grace are ye saved through faith; and that not of yourselves: it is the gift of God: Not of works, lest any man should boast" (Eph. 2:8-9).

Let us look at the ethnic breakdown of mankind on the face of planet earth today. How does God see mankind? There are some misconceptions here, and as a result of these misconceptions, many people are not able to walk in the fullness of what God has provided for them because they are walking in ignorance and not in the knowledge of the Word of God.

Anthropologists have divided mankind into several different ethnic categories, but in the sight of God there are really only three classes of men on the earth. There may be many more as far as the anthropologist is concerned, but we cannot always go by scientific definitions when it comes to spiritual matters. We have to go by the Word of God.

> **Give none offence, neither to the Jews, nor to the Gentiles, nor to the church of God.**
>
> **(1 Cor. 10:32)**

These are the three classes of man on this planet today as far as God is concerned: the Jew, the Gentile and the Church of God. You are either a Jew or a Gentile, or you are the Church of God. The Church of God is made up of both Jews and Gentiles. If you are not in the Church, then you are either a Jew or a

Gentile. If you are not a Gentile, you have to be a Jew, and if you are not a Jew, you have to be a Gentile, or you are in the Body of Christ. This is according to the Word of God! See it for yourself.

I have heard several people make some statements like this: "What about the Fatherhood of God and the brotherhood of man? We are all God's children. We are all brothers and sisters in God."

THAT IS NOT TRUE!

The Fatherhood of God and the brotherhood of man is a concept that has been promulgated through the years. But this concept is incorrect. The only way you are my spiritual brother is if you have the same Father I have. If we do not have the same Father, then we are not brothers or sisters, spiritually speaking. *GOD IS THE CREATOR OF US ALL*, but He is not the *FATHER* of us all. The only way God can be our Father is by way of adoption, and Jesus Christ is the adoption agency. If you do not qualify by being born again, you cannot be adopted into the family of God.

There are some people who think they are being sophisticated by saying, "I don't have to belong to any church. I'm just as much a child of God as the preacher is. We are all the children of God. God is the Father of us all." *NO, WE ARE NOT ALL CHILDREN OF GOD!* We are only children of God when we have accepted Jesus as our Savior and Lord!

"Well, my mamma was a Christian, my great grandfather was a Christian, and my Uncle Joe was a preacher." That does not make you a Christian. If the fact that your mother was a Christian would make you a Christian, then you would be God's grandchild.

31

GOD DOES NOT HAVE ANY GRANDCHILDREN.
He has only sons and daughters.

> **There was a man sent from God, whose name
> was John.** [This is talking about John the Baptist.] **The
> same came for a witness, to bear witness of the Light**
> [referring to Jesus Christ] **that all men through him
> might believe. He was not that Light, but was sent
> to bear witness of that Light. That was the true Light,
> which lighteth every man that cometh into the world.
> He was in the world, and the world was made by him,
> and the world knew him not. He came unto his
> own...** ["Own" meaning Israel because Jesus came
> out of the line of Abraham. So He was actually a
> descendant of Abraham, and the Jews (or what we call
> the "chosen people") had the first opportunity to
> receive Him as Messiah and as Redeemer. They
> rejected Him and this is what Verse 11 is talking about.]
> **He came unto his own, and his own received him not.
> But as many as received him, to them gave he power
> to become the sons of God, even to them that believe
> on his name.**
>
> **(John 1:6-12)**

If He gave the power (authority, right or privilege)
to become a son of God to those who received Him,
then that would mean they were not the sons of God
before that time or it wouldn't have been necessary
for Him to give them the power to become something
they already were.

This tells us very clearly, then, that everyone is
not a son (or a child) of God, and God is not the Father
of every man.

2

THE FATHERHOOD OF GOD AND THE BROTHERHOOD OF MAN?

I want to cover in more depth the subject I began in the preceding chapter concerning *the Fatherhood of God and the brotherhood of man.* I pointed out that we need to realize that the concept of God as the Father of all mankind and the belief that all men are brothers is not biblically correct. The idea may be philosophically sound, but the Bible does not indicate that this is the case.

Granted, it seems reasonable that God would be the Father of us all because He is the Creator of us all. However, "creator" and "father" are two different things. You are not a child of God and God is not your Father until you become His child. The only way you can become God's child is through adoption, and Jesus is the adoption agency. However, there are certain requirements that must be met in order to complete the adoption process.

For example, people adopt children all the time. They don't walk into the adoption agency and say, "I want one of those or one of these." Even though agencies have placed children for adoption and are in need of adopting parents, they still do not indiscriminately give children to people. There are certain parameters prospective parents must meet — certain requirements they must measure up to or else they cannot adopt children.

It is the same with Almighty God. You are not God's child until you are adopted into His family. Once you have been adopted by the Lord, you become what the Bible calls a Christian, then you come under the Law of the New Covenant.

Because it is so important for believers to understand this aspect of what it means to become a Christian, I want to cover supporting Scriptures in the first chapter of John. As I said before, there are many people who are laboring under the illusion that they are children of God because they subscribe to the idea that God is the Father of all mankind. The thing that is so sad about this concept is that they are going to get to the end of the line and find out that their names are not written in the Lamb's Book of Life because they did not go through *the adoption process.*

> **There was a man sent from God, whose name was John. [This is referring to John the Baptist]. The same came for a witness, to bear witness of the Light, that all men through him might believe. He was not that Light, but was sent to bear witness of that Light. That was the true Light, which lighteth every man that cometh into the world.**
>
> **(John 1:6-9)**

Let's take a close look at verse nine, because if you do not understand what this verse is really saying, you might get into some problems. There are those who claim that everyone has a spark of goodness in them, and they use this verse to back this claim up. This "light" is the *"LIGHT OF THE KNOWLEDGE OF GOD,"* and every person who comes into the world has enough of this illumination. We are not talking about *goodness;* we are not talking about a spark of morality — WE ARE TALKING ABOUT A CONSCIOUSNESS AND AN AWARENESS OF THE *PRIME MOVER, GOD ALMIGHTY — THERE IS THAT LIGHT IN EVERY MAN!*

This does not mean that every man is a child of God; this does not mean that every man is going to be saved. *It means that that "LIGHT" is in every man so that no man has any excuse for not believing in God unless that man was born in a way that he could not rationally think or exercise his will.* In cases like that, we have to defer to the mercy and all-knowingness of God. We have to believe that God is not going to get any pleasure out of consigning a creature who is unable to respond to Him to eternal damnation.

I like to go back to the appeal Abraham made to God when God came down and appeared to him and said He was going to do something about Sodom and Gomorrah. Abraham set himself between Sodom and Gomorrah and God by stating, "Peradventure there be fifty righteous within the city: wilt thou also destroy and not spare the place for the fifty righteous that are therein? . . . far from thee to do after this manner, to slay the righteous with the wicked, and that the righteous should be as the wicked, that be far from thee: Shall not the Judge of all the earth do right?" (Gen. 18:24-25). God told Abraham that if He would find ten righteous people, He would spare the city. I think Abraham stopped asking too soon; consequently, he and God could not come up with the required number, so the city was wiped out (Gen. 18:23-32). During this discourse, however, Abraham said something that is important to all of us:

"SHALL NOT THE JUDGE OF ALL THE EARTH DO RIGHT?"

Therefore, for all those people who have something wrong with them from birth that causes them to be unable to make rational decisions, I believe we can trust God in their behalf. At any rate, we are not talking about such people; we are talking about people who have the ability to make rational decisions. We are talking about the ones who know what is right and what is wrong. We are talking about people who have the ability to know there is Someone "out there" who is responsible for all we see around us and that this Supreme Being is worthy of respect, praise and worship.

It is interesting to note that as you study the history of mankind on the earth, anthropologists have not found any cultures, regardless of how ancient or how primitive, that did or do not worship something — be it the sun, the moon, the stars, crocodiles, the river, rats, dogs, cows or whatever. Mankind has a need to worship something outside of himself. Because of this *Light* that is in every man who is born into this world, making him aware of the fact that there is something out there that is bigger than himself to which he owes allegiance, people feel a need to worship.

Until the *light of the glorious gospel of Christ comes to a man,* he will not be able to know that that Light is on the inside; therefore, he will enter into a perversion of that Light, and he will never come to a full understanding of what that Light is, even though it is residing within him. It is only when the light of the gospel comes that man knows what that *Light* is, and he will then be totally satisfied in his *INNER MAN!*

You hear some people say that you cannot prove the existence of God. *ACCORDING TO THE BIBLE, YOU CAN!* However, I will discuss this later so that I can continue on with these particular verses in the Gospel of John.

> **That was the true Light, which lighteth every man that cometh into the world. He was in the world, and the world was made by him, and the world knew him not. He came unto his own, and his own received him not.** [Concerning "his own" — "his" is referring to Jesus; "own" is referring to the nation of Israel. When God made the covenant with Abraham, He told him that out of Abraham's loins He would bring forth the Redeemer, "and unto him shall the gathering of the people be" (Gen. 49:10).]
>
> **(John 1:9-11)**

Because God had a covenant with Abraham in the beginning, God gave Israel "the first right of refusal." In other words, God gave Israel the first opportunity to receive the Redeemer, or to refuse to receive Him.

> **But as many as received him, to them gave he power to become the sons of God.**
>
> **(John 1:12)**

The word "power" in the Greek means, "authority, right or privilege." Evidently, before anyone was given the "authority, right or privilege" to become a son of God, there was no way anyone could become His son. If one could have become a son of God before receiving this "power," it would not have been necessary to give anyone this "authority, right, or privilege."

This immediately shoots down the concept of the Fatherhood of God and the brotherhood of man. This verse clearly lets us know that all people are not children of God.

I know this verse bursts a lot of balloons for people, but we need to call things as they are, and we need to accept the freedom God has given to us in His Word, and not to mix it up with our own concepts.

Notice something else here that is very important. I have had many people say to me, "I believe in God — I have always believed in God, and I have believed in Jesus since I was a little child."

DO YOU KNOW WHAT? You can still go to hell believing that Jesus lived and believing that God is God! You do not get saved believing that Jesus is Jesus or that God is God. The Bible says the demons believe and tremble. They know Jesus is Lord and that He is King of kings. But demons are not saved, are they? Because what goes along with believing is *RECEIVING!* You can believe something and never receive it. And until you receive it, it does not do you any personal good. What you believe, may be true, but your believing does not affect you personally until you receive it. You can sit down at a table full of food and say, ''I believe that if I eat this food it will keep me from starving to death.'' Yet, you can starve to death right in the middle of the fanciest restaurant in the world. Unless you get some food into your body, you can die believing the food will keep you from starving to death.

HOW CAN WE PROVE THE EXISTENCE OF GOD?

For therein is the righteousness of God revealed from faith to faith: as it is written, The just shall live by faith. For the wrath of God is revealed from heaven against all ungodliness and unrighteousness of men, who hold the truth in unrighteousness. Because that which may be known of God is manifest in them; for God hath shewed it unto them. For the invisible things of him [the unseen things of God] from the creation of the world are clearly seen, being understood by the things that are made, even his eternal power and Godhead; so that they are without excuse.

(Rom. 1:17-20)

This is saying, ''Yes, God is invisible, but the world and the universe He created are visible. *The way you know God exists is by the VISIBLE UNIVERSE and the WORLD He created,* and God says we are without excuse in not recognizing Him and His sovereign power.

WHAT ARE SOME OF THE INVISIBLE THINGS OF GOD?

His power, His creativity, His beauty, His wisdom, His intelligence, His orderliness — these are just a few of the attributes of God we cannot see with our eyes, but we see the *RESULTS* of these attributes, don't we?

> **For the invisible things of him from the creation of the world** [notice the next three words] *are clearly seen.*
> **(Rom. 1:20, italics mine)**

It does not say they are obscure; it says, ''. . . *they are clearly seen. . . .* '' The only person who would not see them is someone who is deaf, dumb, blind or dishonest.

It does not say, ''clearly perceived,'' leaving it up to some kind of rationale of your mind. Paul says, *SEEN,* and anyone who is not blind can see that this is a physical world — you can see it, touch it, feel it and smell it.

> **For the invisible things of him from the creation of the world are clearly seen,** *being understood by the things that are made. . . .*
> **(Rom. 1:20, italics mine)**

What are the ''things that are made''? The earth, the sun, the moon, the stars — the whole universe. ''. . . *even his eternal power. . . .* '' It took some power to make this universe. It took some power to create this world, and it takes some power to keep all the stars and planets and suns and galaxies all working perfectly without any hindrance and without any mess-ups. Everything works as it is supposed to work, just as God designed it.

WE HAVE NO EXCUSE!

No one can get up in front of the High Tribunal and try to argue God down, ''Well, you know if I had seen you, I would have believed in you.'' God says we (meaning the whole of mankind) are without excuse. We can see the world around us, we can see the universe around us, so we do not have any excuse!

Now let us get back to our subject concerning the Church and the Mosaic Law. I like taking these side trips, because I believe they help us to understand more clearly the topic at hand.

Every person who has received Christ, based on believing in Him and every person who has received Him and confessed Him as Lord is considered the Church — a Christian — a part of the Body of Christ. This means he is now classified by God as being neither a Jew nor a Gentile. At one time he was a Gentile, but once he left the Gentile state and became a Christian, he no longer is a part of the Gentile world. It is the same way with the Jew. If a Jew receives Christ as his or her Savior, then he or she is no longer a part of the Jewish world. Let's look at this from the standpoint of the Gentiles, Since the majority of the readers of this book will be of non-Jewish origin.

In the Book of Ephesians, there is a passage that gives indication that the Church — the Christian — is not under the Mosaic Law, and never was. In fact, the Gentiles who are not Christians today are not even under the Mosaic Law or the Ten Commandments.

I have seen incidents of a church recruiting children from the local community who were not even saved and bringing them to Sunday school to try to teach them about keeping the Ten Commandments. You cannot teach a dead person anything. If you think you can, go to the nearest cemetery of your choice and let us see you teach someone who is buried there. Now that may sound comical; however, the point I am making is that you cannot teach someone until that person has life. People have to be alive in order to be able to teach them. Spiritually dead people cannot be taught the Word of God because the Word is spiritually understood. What these children needed was salvation, not teaching. They needed to know about Jesus. Once they accepted Jesus as their Savior, they could be taught the Word of God — not the Ten Commandments, not the Law of Moses, because as Gentiles, they never were under the Law of Moses or the Ten Commandments.

For example, usually the same law of any city, state, government or nation that gives you penalties for breaking the law also has corresponding benefits for keeping the law. In other words, for doing what the law says, there are benefits that accrue to you, just as there are penalties that accrue to you for breaking the law.

If God required the Gentiles to keep the Law of Moses, which included the Ten Commandments, the Law of the Sabbath, etc., then by the same token all the blessings of the Law should also be theirs. Then tell me why there is so much sickness and disease among the Gentile world, when one of the benefits of keeping the Law was freedom from disease? God promised those who kept the Law that He would take sickness from their midst and the number of their days He would fulfill (Exod. 23:25-26). So, if the Gentiles were to keep the Law, then they should be getting the benefits. The reason they don't is because they have nothing to do with the Law.

GENTILES VS. THE CHURCH OF GOD

Before we start our discussion of Ephesians 2, I want to establish to whom Paul is writing this epistle.

> **Paul, an apostle of Jesus Christ by the will of God, to the saints which are at Ephesus, and to the faithful in Christ Jesus.**
>
> **(Eph. 1:1)**

(Geographically speaking, of course, this letter was written to the Christians at Ephesus; however, if the Christians at Ephesus are Christians in the same Body of Christ we are in, and God is their heavenly Father, then the Law should work for us, as well as for them, even though they were in Ephesus and we are in another part of the world.) If we are citizens of the United States, the Constitution supposedly gives us the same privileges whether we are in New York or in California.

Now you may come into conflict with some local laws, but the nation's constitutional laws are governed the same way everywhere by the same Supreme Court, no matter where we live in America.

So, whether this is talking about the saints at Ephesus some 2,000 years ago or the saints in the United States during this present time, it does not make any difference, because we are all a part of the Body of Christ.

Since we have established that Paul is writing to Christians everywhere at all times, let us go on to the second Chapter of Ephesians.

> **Wherefore remember, that ye being in time past Gentiles in the flesh, who are called Uncircumcision by that which is called the Circumcision in the flesh made by hands.**
>
> **(Eph. 2:11)**

We immediately see that these Ephesian Christians had been Gentiles because Ephesus was basically a Gentile city, rather than a Jewish one. If Paul had been writing this letter to Jerusalem, he more than likely would have said, "that ye being in time past Israelites in the flesh," because Jerusalem is a Jewish place.

But here he says, "Wherefore remember, that ye being in time past Gentiles" — apparently, they were no longer considered Gentiles. They were now considered the Body of Christ, or Christians.

In the Book of Genesis, we are told how God established a covenant with Abraham. In that covenant, God gave Abraham a sign or a seal of that covenant, which was *circumcision*. After a male child was eight days old, he was to have the foreskin of his penis removed surgically. It was a peculiar sign; we have no record that anyone else as a nation in the world had circumcision as a sign of a covenant — only the nation of Israel. Consequently, many times when others would refer to these covenant people (who were also known as Hebrews, Jews, Chosen People or Israelites), they would sometimes call them *"the*

44

circumcision.'' Therefore, whenever anyone heard someone talking about *''the circumcision,''* that person would know he was talking about the Hebrews or Israelites. The Jews, on the other hand, because they had this peculiar covenant seal, which no one else had, would refer to the rest of the world as *''the uncircumcised or uncircumcision.''* Instead of using the term ''Gentile,'' they would say, ''the uncircumcision,'' and anyone listening would know they were talking about non-Jews. *This is what is being discussed in the latter part of the eleventh verse of Ephesians 2.* Now let's look at verse 12:

> **That at that time ye were without Christ, being aliens from the commonwealth of Israel, and strangers from the covenants of promise, having no hope, and without God in the world.**
>
> **(Eph. 2:12)**

Notice, they were called *aliens* and *strangers* to the covenant. WAIT A MINUTE, if they were strangers to the Covenant, how could they be expected to keep the Law of the Covenant? That means the Gentiles are not under the Law, and neither is the Church.

Let's take another step to enable us to confirm this. Any man who has not received Christ as his Savior is outside of the family of God. Therefore, when he or she dies, he or she will go to hell. Many people do not like to talk about hell, but it does not bother me to do so, because I do not plan to go there. There are some people who get upset about the gas chamber. They can have a gas chamber on every corner; it does not bother me because I do not plan to ever be in one. I plan to obey the law so I won't have to go.

Consequently, I am not going to waste any time arguing about whether gas chambers are right, or whether capital punishment is right. Don't commit any capital crime, then you will not have to worry about capital punishment.

Many people have the idea that hell is a place where God is going to send you at the end because you did not do a certain thing.

NO, NO, NO!

YOU ARE ALREADY ON YOUR WAY TO HELL IF YOU ARE OUTSIDE OF CHRIST! There is only one reason for a person to go to hell — only one sin that gets a man into hell! Think of a man being the biggest anything bad you can imagine (a murderer, whoremonger, dope addict, dope peddler, rapist, hitman, abortionist — whatever bad you can name — he is it).

Then, on the other hand, think of how good a person can be (sweet, kind, nice, law-abiding, moral, never does anything wrong, never has a bad thought — just a good, moral person). Do you know that when both of these men come to the end of their lives, both will end up in hell — they both will end up the very same way? It doesn't make any difference how they have lived — whether good or bad.

IT IS NOT WHAT YOU DO OR DON'T DO THAT GETS YOU INTO HELL!

You only go to hell for one sin! And that sin is found in the Gospel of John 16, beginning at verse 7. This is Jesus Christ himself speaking:

> **Nevertheless I tell you the truth; It is expedient** [or necessary] **for you that I go away: for if I go not away, the Comforter** [or the Holy Spirit] **will not come unto you; but if I depart, I will send him unto you. And when he is come, he will reprove the world of sin, and of righteousness, and of judgment. Of sin, because they believe not on me.**
>
> **(John 16:7-9)**

THAT IS THE SIN!

Not believing on Jesus is the only sin that gets one into hell. Of course, believing on Him implies receiving Him according to John 1:12. It is the whole concept of believing and receiving and confessing Christ as Lord. If you don't confess Christ as Lord, then you reject the love of God offered through His Son.

Think about it! What greater sin could you commit than to reject the love of Almighty God? Jesus himself told us, "For God so loved the world, that he gave his only begotten Son, that whosoever believeth in him should not perish, but have everlasting life" (John 3:16). If you reject God's provision, that is the one sin that will get you into hell.

Some folks think they are earning their way into heaven by keeping the Law of Moses and keeping the Ten Commandments, and by going to church on Saturdays or by following this or that tradition. THEY ARE WRONG! *The Bible says you go to heaven because you accept Christ, or you go to hell because you reject Him!* AND THAT IS THE WAY IT IS!

3

THE WORK OF THE HOLY SPIRIT

Let us look again at what Jesus says about those who are going to be rejected and those who are going to be accepted by Him.

> **Nevertheless I tell you the truth; It is expedient** [or necessary] **for you that I go away: for if I go not away, the Comforter** [or the Holy Spirit] **will not come unto you; but if I depart, I will send him unto you. And when he is come, he will reprove the world of SIN....**
>
> (John 16:7-8)

Notice that it says "S-I-N" and not "S-I-N-S." Some people think that if they do this or they don't do that, they commit sin. For example, it is a common belief that if a person commits suicide, he or she will automatically go to hell. Where is that found in the Bible? It simply is not there. Suicide is not going to get you into hell. Suicide is going to get you into the grave. You will not go to hell any quicker for committing suicide than you would for committing rape, or murder, or fornication or any other sin. It is not those individual things that put people in hell. These passages of Scripture very clearly delineate what puts people in hell.

Of sin, BECAUSE THEY BELIEVE NOT ON ME.
(John 16:9, emphasis mine)

That is the sin that puts people in hell — not accepting Jesus as their personal Savior and Lord. It is not that God is going to arbitrarily punish you because you do not become a Christian.

JESUS IS THE ONLY WAY OUT!

And if you do not accept the only way out, what else is there for you? If a building is on fire and burning down, the roof is about to cave in, and there is only one door out and you do not go out that door, tell me how are you going to get out of the building? You are not! *Well, Jesus is the way out of sin.* If you do not accept Him, you cannot get away from the condemnation sins bring. It is not that God is standing over you with a gun, demanding that you accept His Son, it is just that that is the way the system is designed. *The only exit route is Jesus,* so if you do not accept Him, there is no way out for you, and you will go to hell!

Of course, the other things are wrong, they are bad and Christians should not do them, but they are not the things that will take you to hell. Your good works or lack of good works will not get you into heaven or hell, *IT IS ACCEPTING OR REJECTING JESUS THAT DOES IT!*

When I tell people this truth, I have had some individuals come up to me later and say, ''What about the blasphemy of the Holy Ghost?''

WHAT IS THE PURPOSE AND JOB OF THE HOLY SPIRIT?

The primary work of the Holy Spirit is to bear witness to the fact that Jesus Christ is the Son of God and the Savior of all mankind. How does the Holy Spirit bear witness to that fact? He does it through the the ministry gifts Jesus has set in the Church, such as: Apostles, Prophets, Evangelists, Pastors and Teachers.

As these ministry gifts operate under the anointing of the Holy Spirit (preaching or teaching Jesus Christ and His Word), they give testimony to the world concerning the reality of Jesus.

The Bible says he who blasphemes against the Holy Ghost has neither forgiveness in this world nor in the world to come. You know why? It is because as I mentioned before — there is only one exit out of the burning building. If you do not take the exit door out, you cannot get out, so you are going to burn up in the building. *The blasphemy of the Holy Ghost is to reject the Holy Ghost's testimony concerning Jesus as being the way, the truth and the life!* If you do not accept that testimony, how are you going to get saved? You can't!

Someone might say, "Well, I did not vote." A "no vote" is the same as a vote against. You either are for Jesus or against Him — there is no in between — and it is you who must make the choice.

WHAT DID THE EARLY CHURCH HAVE TO SAY ABOUT KEEPING THE LAW?

Let us move on to the Book of Acts 15, and see what the early church said about the Law of Moses, about the Sabbath days, about the Ten Commandments, about circumcision, etc.

Let's start at the beginning of the Church Age, which is the beginning of our age. We are in the same Church that Peter, James, John and the rest of the original Apostles were in. *There is only one Church.* So let us start at the beginning of this Church age and find out how the founding fathers dealt with this matter of keeping the Law. If what we do today is consistent with what they did in the beginning, then what the Bible says has to satisfy every preacher, every theologian, every denomination, every church and every member in the Body of Christ.

> **And certain men which came down from Judaea taught the brethren, and said, Except ye be circumcised after the manner of Moses, ye cannot be saved.**
>
> **(Acts 15:1)**

Notice how they related salvation to keeping the Law of Moses. There are people today who will tell you that if you do not go to church on Saturday, you cannot be saved. If you do not keep the Sabbath, you cannot be saved. If you do not abstain from eating certain kinds of foods, you cannot be saved. They were saying this over 2,000 years ago also, and we have men who are saying the same thing in this very day and time.

Circumcision was a sign, a covenant sign, that God gave to Abraham, and then to Isaac, and then to Jacob and his twelve sons. It was given to the nation of Israel. It was not given to the Gentiles. It certainly was not given to the Church, because the Church was not even there at that time.

And certain men which came down from Judaea taught the brethren, and said, Except ye be circumcised after the manner of Moses, ye cannot be saved. [These men were saying that salvation was based on works because it is a work to circumcise and be circumcised. This teaching was in direct opposition to Ephesians 2:8-9, which teaches that salvation is a gift of God and is to be received by faith.] **When therefore Paul and Barnabas had no small dissension and disputation with them, they determined that Paul and Barnabas, and certain other of them, should go up to Jerusalem unto the apostles and elders about this question.** [They had a question about this matter. They needed to go up to Jerusalem because that was where the mother church was located and where the apostles were residing. You see, we are not unique in having questions. These men who had walked and talked with Jesus, who knew Him intimately, had questions.] **And being brought on their way by the church, they passed through Phenice and Samaria, declaring the conversion of the Gentiles: and they caused great joy unto all the brethren. And when they were come to Jerusalem, they were received of the church, and of the apostles and elders, and they declared all that God had done with them. But there rose up certain of the sect of the Pharisees which believed, saying, That it was needful to circumcise them, and to command them to keep the law of Moses. And the apostles and elders came together for to consider of this matter. And when there had been much disputing, Peter rose up, and said unto them, Men and brethren, you know how that a good while ago God made choice among us, that the Gentiles by my mouth should hear the word of the gospel, and believe. And God, which knoweth the hearts, bare**

them witness, giving them the Holy Ghost, even as he did unto us; [Notice here that Peter is making a distinction between the Jew and the Gentile. He was himself a Jew, and he told of how God gave opportunity for the Gentiles to receive the Word through him, a Jew. It was Jews who were in the upper room on the Day of Pentecost — not Gentiles.] **And put no difference between us and them, purifying their hearts by faith. Now therefore why tempt ye God, to put a yoke upon the neck of the disciples, which neither our fathers nor we were able to bear?**
(Acts 15:1-10)

They called the Law of Moses a yoke! And that is exactly what it was. The reason it was a yoke was because before the time of Jesus no one could be born again. Mankind was spiritually dead, cut off and alienated from God, and the only way God could deal with them was in an outward, physical, tangible way.

The Lord gave the Jews this outward law to give them something to shoot for until Jesus came with righteousness for those who would receive Him. Through their obedience to following that Law (as best they could), God accounted their obedience for righteousness.

Peter called the Law a yoke. He said their fathers (predecessors) could not keep it, they couldn't keep it, so why put the Law on the Gentiles?

But we believe that through the grace of the Lord Jesus Christ we shall be saved, even as they. Then all the multitude kept silence, and gave audience to Barnabas and Paul, declaring what miracles and wonders God had wrought among the Gentiles by

them. And after they had held their peace, James answered, saying, Men and brethren, hearken unto me: Simeon hath declared how God at the first did visit the Gentiles, to take out of them a people for his name. And to this agree the words of the prophets; as it is written, After this I will return, and will build again the tabernacle of David, which is fallen down; and I will build again the ruins thereof, and I will set it up: That the residue of men might seek after the Lord, and all the Gentiles, upon who my name is called, saith the Lord, who doeth all these things. Known unto God are all his works from the beginning of the world. Wherefore my sentence is, that we trouble not them, which from among the Gentiles are turned to God. [This is talking about us, the Christian, non-Jews, who have turned to God.] But that we write unto them, that they abstain from pollutions of idols, and from fornication, and from things strangled, and from blood. For Moses of old time hath in every city them that preach him, being read in the synagogues every sabbath day. Then pleased it the apostles and elders, with the whole church, to send chosen men of their own company to Antioch with Paul and Barnabas; namely, Judas surnamed Barnabas, and Silas, chief men among the brethren: And they wrote letters by them after this manner; The apostles and elders and brethren send greeting unto the brethren which are of the Gentiles in Antioch and Syria and Cilicia: Forasmuch as we have heard, that certain which went out from us have troubled you with words, subverting your souls, saying, Ye must be circumcised, and keep the law: to whom we gave no such commandment. [There is no one standing in any pulpit in this nation or anywhere else in the world today whom God has told to tell anyone that he must be circumcised or that he or she is to keep the Law of Moses in order to be saved. If God did command this by the Holy Spirit today, He would be in contradiction to His own Word, and the Bible says that God is not

confused, nor can He lie or contradict himself. Therefore, no one has a right to demand that anyone keep the Law of Moses today when they expressly did not do it at the beginning of the Church Age!] **It seemed good unto us, being assembled with one accord, to send chosen men unto you with our beloved Barnabas and Paul, Men that have hazarded their lives for the name of our Lord Jesus Christ. We have sent therefore Judas and Silas, who shall also tell you the same things by mouth. For it seemed good to the Holy Ghost, and to us, to lay upon you no greater burden than these necessary things;** [These men claimed that this was the word from the Holy Ghost. Now if what the Holy Ghost said satisfied them, guess what? It had better satisfy you, and the first you-know-what church, down on the corner of you-know-what street and avenue. IT HAS TO SATISFY THEM! If it satisfies the Holy Ghost, friend, it has to satisfy us!] **That ye abstain from meats offered to idols, and from blood, and from things strangled, and from fornication: from which if ye keep yourselves, ye shall do well. Fare ye well.**
(Acts 15:11-29)

That is the end of their letter. That is the end of their communication. Notice what is conspicuous in its absence, and that is that they said nothing about keeping the Sabbath day. They said nothing about circumcision, they said nothing about following the Ten Commandments. They said nothing about keeping the Law of Moses. HOW READEST THOU? Who are you going to believe? The First Church on Second Avenue on so-and-so boulevard? The so-and-so denomination? Or the Bible? I hope you took time to read this in your own Bible. If you cannot trust your own Bible, you need to get rid of it and get one you can trust.

There is a passage in the Old Testament that "adds fuel to the fire" and supports what we have already covered concerning the Law of Moses and the keeping of the Ten Commandments.

DO YOU KNOW THAT THERE ARE EVIL SPIRITS IN THE WORLD TODAY?

Whether you are aware of them or not, whether you believe in them or not is irrelevant and immaterial. *They do exist.* There are sex spirits, there are homosexual spirits, lying spirits, fornicating spirits, and whether you know it or not, there are religious spirits. That is why sometimes you see people who take hold of something which is as wrong as a three-dollar bill, and yet they will not let go. These individuals seem to be so tied to their beliefs that you cannot cut them loose with a razor blade. The thing or thought just seems to engulf them, and you wonder how some people who appear so intelligent cannot see what the Word of God clearly reveals. *It is because they are blinded by religious spirits.* Satan has sent these spirits out into the world to cause confusion, so that people do not know which way to go or what to believe. THE HOLY GHOST IS NOT CONFUSED. He would not make fifteen different denominations and everyone of them say something different, causing people to be doubtful and confused.

I am not implying that every individual who started or had anything to do with the beginning of a denomination had something wrong with him. What I am saying is that people can be influenced by spirits without even knowing it. Spirits are very clever. They will make you think you thought the thing up, that you got it right from the Holy Ghost, so it must be right. But if the Holy Ghost is working in me, and the Holy Ghost is working in you, and the Holy Ghost is working in someone else, we are not going to come out with five different denominations. No way! People are confused and they are confused by religious spirits.

"Well, which denomination is right?" I will tell you which one is right. *THE B-I-B-L-E, THAT IS THE ONE THAT IS RIGHT.* If you stick with the Bible, you cannot go wrong.

> **Wherefore the children of Israel shall keep the sabbath, to observe the sabbath throughout their generations, for a perpetual covenant. It is a sign between me and the children of Israel for ever....**
> **(Exod. 31:16)**

The word "forever," when used in the Bible, does not mean forever in the sense of eternity. Because if it were going to be the Sabbath forever, it would have to include the total Law which had to do with the animal sacrifices and everything else. And those sacrifices are over, because Jesus is the "Lamb slain from the foundation of the world." So when it says "forever," I believe this was the strongest term God could use for the Jews to understand how long something was to be in operation. It did not mean forever in the sense of eternal, but rather it meant "for ever as long as you are alive" the covenant is to be kept. If it meant that the Jews were to keep the Sabbath throughout eternity, then that would mean the Law and everything connected with it would have to go into eternity, and that is not true.

It is a sign between me and the CHILDREN OF ISRAEL....

I want you to notice that God did not say, "It is a sign between me and the GENTILES." He did not say, "It is a sign between me and the Christian." He did not say, "It is a sign between me and the Church." *No, God said it was a sign between Him and the children of Israel!* Christians are not the children of Israel. We are the children of God. Therefore, we, as Christians, are not obligated to keep the Sabbath or anything connected with it!

There are many Christians who are walking in bondage today — bound because of a sincere and honest desire to please God. They are following religious traditions that were either passed down to them from their parents or because of exposure to certain teachings they received at church or Sunday school.

As an informed believer, you may be able to help these people. You may be the channel to set them free. A true minister of the gospel might never have an opportunity to speak to them, but you might be the catalyst that God can use to help them get free from religious bondage.

There are many churches today telling people they cannot be saved if they wear jewelry; they can't be saved if they don't go to church on Saturday; they can't be saved if they don't do this or that. People need to find out for themselves what God has to say about all this rather than what the preacher, the bishop, the Pope or anybody else has to say.

According to the Scriptures we read in the Book of Acts, there were certain things Christians were asked to do. Let's look at that portion of Acts 15 again:

> **Wherefore my sentence is, that we trouble not them, which from among the Gentiles are turned to God** [this is talking about Christians]: **But that we write unto them, that they abstain from** [number one] **POLLUTIONS OF IDOLS. . . .**
>
> **(Acts 15:19-20)**

At the time when God called Abraham and then Isaac and then Jacob (who later was called Israel) and then Jacob's twelve sons, the world was polytheistic. The people had a multiplicity of gods whom they worshiped. The Jew was the only one during that time who was unique in that he was monotheistic — he worshiped only one God. All the Gentiles had once been heathenistic or paganistic. They worshiped animals, the sun, the moon and idols made with men's hands from stone, wood, etc. They were *polluted* with the worship of idols. The apostles in Acts 15:20 were letting these Gentiles who had now become Christians know that they had to put aside these polytheistic gods and worship only the one true and living God.

> . . . [secondly] **from FORNICATION. . . .**
>
> **(Acts 15:20)**

Fornication means sexual intercourse outside of marriage. It means the same thing today that it meant some 2,000 years ago.

...[thirdly] **and from things STRANGLED....**
(Acts 15:20)

When God set up the Law at Mount Sinai with Moses and then gave the children of Israel His decree for them to observe the Law, they also were told to bring different kinds of animals and different kinds of sacrifices to atone for different kinds of sin. But their animals were always to be killed with a knife or something of that nature, and the blood was to be drained from the carcasses.

In the pagan world, it was quite different. Instead of killing an animal with a blade of some sort, they would strangle the animal — choke the animal to death — and in many cases, they would then offer the animal in sacrifice. Sometimes the priests would punch holes in the animal's carcass, drain the blood and then drink it. That may sound strange to us, but in some parts of the world they still do that to this day. There are certain areas of the world where people eat what is called "blood sausages" — sausages that are full of the blood of the animal the sausage is made from.

...[fourthly] **and from BLOOD.**

(Acts 15:20)

God said, "the life of the flesh is in the blood" (Lev. 17:11). Consequently, man was not supposed to drink the blood of another living thing. However, in pagan worship and sacrifice, people did. They felt there was something mystical about drinking the blood of a sacrificed animal and certain powers were granted to the imbiber.

God's children are never to drink blood, according to the New Covenant because the one sacrifice for time and eternity is the Lord Jesus Christ. He has already died; He has already risen; He has already ascended, and no one else ever needs to make another blood sacrifice because divine justice has been eternally satisfied.

THE LIFE OF CHRIST IN THE LIFE OF THE BELIEVER!

How do we know that Jesus Christ is a person? How do we know that He died on Calvary? How do we know that He ascended into heaven? How do we know that He is coming back again? HOW DO WE KNOW THESE THINGS? BY FAITH IN THE WORD OF GOD — the Bible — that is how!

The apostles who walked with Jesus did not believe the Bible. The Bible was not even written then. How could they believe it? Our faith is based on the Word of God. That is the reason why I harp on the Word so much. That is why I stay on it, because everything we believe concerning spiritual matters is predicated on the Word. The reason why many Christians are missing out on the things of God is because they are waiting for a feeling. They have been going by an emotion, and their prayer life, their Bible reading, their commitment to Christ are all predicated on some kind of feeling.

In fact, these Christians can be described by the words of an old song: *"Every time I feel the Spirit moving in my heart, I will pray."* And some of them have not felt the Spirit moving in twenty years, so they have not prayed.

Don't misunderstand me. I am not saying that you will not have some feelings. I am not saying feelings will not come when you pray, but if you wait until you have a feeling in order to pray, YOU WILL NOT PRAY AS OFTEN AS YOU SHOULD! Satan will see to that — he will see to it that your feelings don't come. *No, you pray because the Word says to pray without ceasing.*

Some Christians are waiting to get the "Bible-reading" feeling, and then they will study the Scriptures. They don't understand that they are supposed to read the Bible because the Word says, "Study to shew thyself approved unto God, a workman that needeth not to be ashamed" (2 Tim. 2:15).

As I stated before, the faith of the apostles when they walked with Christ during His earthly ministry was based on their senses. Our faith is based on the Word of God. If you base your faith on anything other than the Word, you are going to be up the creek in a boat with no oars.

> Moreover, brethren, I declare unto you the gospel which I preached unto you, which also ye have received, and wherein ye stand: By which also ye are saved, if ye keep in memory what I preached unto you, unless ye have believed in vain. For I delivered unto you first of all that which I also received, how that Christ died for our sins according to the scriptures; And that he was buried, and that he rose again the third day according to the scriptures.
>
> (1 Cor. 15:1-4)

"According to the Scriptures" — the Word — not according to a feeling, but according to the Word!

When Jesus walked the earth, some of the people believed He was the prophet Moses had talked about.

Moses had said that in the latter days God would raise up a prophet for the Jews like himself and that unto him would be the gathering of the people. This was, of course, referring to Jesus. Some thought Jesus was the Son of God. Some even went so far as to accept Him as the Messiah, but they did not believe He had died for them or was going to rise again for their justification. As I said before, no one could experience righteousness until after Jesus' resurrection.

The Bible says all have sinned and come short of the glory of God (Rom. 3:23); and every man who is outside of Christ (whether Jew or Gentile) is spiritually dead. Spiritual death does not mean non-existence. In other words, when we think of something as being dead in the English language, we think of the thing as being non-existent. Spiritual death means a life apart from God. As far as God is concerned, for the spiritually dead person, it is as though he does not exist. I have used this illustration before, but I think it is apropos and it gets the point across.

I am sure you have heard the term ''color blind.'' What does it mean when we say a person is color blind? It means that certain colors do not register on that person's optic nerve. It does not mean that he cannot see or that he is totally blind; it simply means he cannot distinguish certain colors.

Spiritual death is like being color blind. When a man is color blind, he can see, but he cannot see a particular color. When a man is spiritually dead, he is alive, but he is dead to God. The spiritually dead man is considered color blind as far as God is concerned. He looks in God's direction, but his ''spiritual'' optic nerve does not see God, just as the color-blind man's optic nerve does not see a particular color.

THE SPIRITUALLY DEAD MAN DOES NOT NEED FORGIVENESS OF SINS!

If God forgave the sinner of his sins, it would not do him any good. He would still go to hell. UNDERSTAND WHAT I AM TALKING ABOUT, AND READ THE FOLLOWING VERY CAREFULLY OR YOU WILL GET CONFUSED ON THIS POINT! Most people think God is forgiving sinners of their sins. *(I am talking very technically now, so follow me carefully.)*

When a sinner comes to Christ, God forgives him of his sins, generally speaking. But technically speaking, when a man accepts Christ as his Savior, *God does not FORGIVE his sins, what God does is to REMIT his sins which means HE WIPES OUT THE MAN'S TOTAL PAST AS THOUGH IT NEVER EXISTED.* In fact, the day when a man accepts Christ is just as if the man were born that day. All those years, all the way back to the date of his physical birth, are wiped out!

The sins God forgives are the sins of Christians. If I commit a sin, I say, "Father, I have sinned; forgive me." And He forgives me. But for the sinner, his sins are remitted — wiped out. It is as if the sinner has a brand-new start. When a Christian sins, he does not get a brand-new start, because he is the same person he was before the sin — he is still a child of God. He just keeps right on being in the family of God. It is as though he just made a mistake. When God forgives him, God just erases that mistake.

The sinner does not need forgiveness of sin. What the sinner needs is a *NEW NATURE!* He needs a nature that is spiritually alive. He needs to be able to see God like the color-blind man needs to be able to see all the colors there are. The sinner needs to become a new creature in Christ Jesus. If you do not become a new creature, you are condemned, and you can keep the Sabbath day all you want — it will not make any difference.

> **Therefore if any man be in Christ, he is a new creature** [or new creation]: **old things are passed away; behold, all things are become new.**
>
> **(2 Cor. 5:17)**

THIS NEW CREATURE IN CHRIST

He has a brand-new nature! He has a brand-new heart that is implanted and filled with the *agape* kind of love, and the law that he will respond to is the *Law of Love* — not the Ten Commandments, not the Law of Moses, not circumcision, not the Sabbath day, but the Law of Love!

What are the old things that pass away? They surely could not be anything in the physical, because if you are bald-headed the day before you get saved, you are bald-headed the day after. If you have freckles on your nose the day before, you have those same freckles the day after. *The things that pass away are not physical things* — they are spiritual things. The old things that pass away are: spiritual death, alienation, separation, degradation and condemnation. They are all wiped out! What is new? *We are children of God. God is our Father. Jesus is our Elder Brother. The Holy Ghost*

66

is our power source. The Word of God becomes our Sword and agape love becomes our law!

Glory to God, condemnation goes out the window, unrighteousness goes out of the window. I am a new creature in Christ Jesus, and I have a right to enter the Throne Room of God.

IT IS A SPIRITUAL TRANSACTION!

And it has nothing to do with keeping the Law of Moses. It doesn't have anything to do with going to church on the Sabbath, and it has nothing to do with circumcision.

Let us look at a companion Scripture that will help you see this more clearly. This is Jesus speaking, and in the third chapter of John, He says:

> **Jesus answered and said unto him** ["unto him" means to the man Nicodemus who came to Jesus for teaching and instruction], **Verily, verily I say unto thee, Except a man be born again, he cannot see the kingdom of God.** [The word "see" does not refer to visual sight with your physical eyes. Jesus is talking about something spiritual; consequently, what is literally being said is this: "Except a man be born again, he cannot come to know the kingdom of God." Everyone who has not yet accepted Christ is in the natural. Jesus is in the spiritual. So you have to make a transfer from the natural to the spiritual, and the way you do that is through the new birth.] **Nicodemus saith unto him, How can a man be born when he is old? can he enter the second time into his mother's womb, and be born?** [Nicodemus thought Jesus was talking about something physical.] **Jesus answered, Verily, verily, I say unto thee, Except a man be born of water and of the Spirit, he cannot enter into the kingdom of God.**

First, Jesus said that unless you are born again, you cannot come to know the Kingdom. Then He says, "Except you are born again, you cannot ENTER into it. When He says "water and Spirit," I want to clarify what He is talking about.

The word "water" does not mean water baptism. The word "water" here is being used symbolically for the Word of God. When Jesus told the parable of the sower, He said a sower went out to sow some seed, and some seed fell by the wayside and the fowls came down and plucked up the seed. Then, later on, when He gave the interpretation of the story, He said that "the seed is the Word." So the word "seed" or the word "water" here are symbols standing for the Word of God.

It takes the Word of God and the Holy Spirit of God to cause the new birth. It takes the Holy Spirit of God and the Word of God to create a new creature in Christ Jesus. In other words, it takes two things to make spiritual life, just like it takes two things to make physical life. It takes a sperm coming in contact with an egg, called fertilization, to cause conception to take place, and a child to be born out of his mother's womb into the world.

The spiritual birth is on this wise. The Spirit of God and the Word of God (the sperm and the egg) come together and conception takes place and a new creature is born out of the world into Christ Jesus. That is spiritual birth. The ground in which the seed is planted is the human heart. The way it gets there is through the preaching of the Word because faith comes by hearing and hearing by the Word of God. So the new birth, then, is the rebirth of the human spirit. It is a spiritual transaction, and not a physical one.

> **Marvel not that I said unto thee, Ye must be born again.** [There is no option. If you want to enter into the family of God, you have to do it by the new birth.]
> **(John 3:7)**

You can keep the Ten Commandments or attempt to keep them all you want, and you can go to church every Sabbath day that comes up, but those things are not going to ingratiate you with God. You have to follow the plan, the prescribed method, and that method is the *new birth.*

4

THE NEW CREATION

Let's cover more Scripture concerning the word "water," not meaning "water baptism." In Ephesians 5, beginning at verse 24, Paul tells us:

> Therefore as the church is subject unto Christ, so let the wives be to their own husbands in every thing. Husbands, love your wives, even as Christ also loved the church, and gave himself for it; That he might sanctify and cleanse it with the washing of water by the word.
>
> (Eph. 5:24-26)

Paul here is using the word "water" as a symbol for the Word of God. All throughout the Bible, you will find different expressions used to describe the Word. For instance, in the Old Testament, it says, "Thy word is like a hammer" (Jer. 23:29). As a hammer breaks up the rocks, so the Word of God breaks up the fallow ground of human hearts.

The prophet Jeremiah also said that God's Word was like a fire shut up in his bones (Jer. 20:9). The Word burns like a fire burns; however, the prophet was using fire symbolically.

Most of the people who attempt to live by the Law do not believe in the New Creation. If they did, they

71

would not try to force this business about the Law, the Ten Commandments and all the other things that passed away when the ''New Creation'' came into being on Christians. *They would know that being born again is the key for getting into the kingdom.*

There are those who believe that the New Birth comes at the Second Coming of Christ. There are some who believe that when you die, you go to sleep. They refer to this as ''soul sleep.'' They say that when you die, you simply go to sleep, and you stay asleep in the grave until Jesus comes back. Then you become born again. According to this belief, it is like being given a second chance. Friend, guess what? *There is no second chance!*

YOU ONLY HAVE ONE CHANCE!

Our one chance is in this life! If we all could get a second chance, then why even be bothered with doing what we are doing now? Why even preach the gospel? Why go to church? After all, you are going to get a second chance anyway. So just wait until the end: eat, drink, and be merry — because you are going to get a second chance.

NO WAY! *This is it!* The Bible tells us, ''To day if ye will hear his voice, harden not your heart'' (Heb. 4:17). Now is the accepted time! If you are not a believer in Jesus now, that means you are unsaved. If you are unsaved, you cannot understand the Word of God. That is why those who subscribe to ''soul sleep'' are locked into keeping the Law. What they are trying to do is to be accepted by God on their own merits. If you are not born again now, you are outside of the family of God. You are going to hell! You hear people say all the time, "I just don't believe in hell." So what? What does that have to do with the fact that hell exists. That is probably what the rich man thought in the story Jesus told concerning the beggar, Lazarus, who sat at the rich man's gate until they both died. The Bible says that *in hell* the rich man lifted up his eyes (Luke 16:20-31).

I hear this all the time, too, "That's what I say about them preachers. They're always trying to use scare tactics, talking about hell." *We are not trying to scare you; WE ARE TRYING TO WARN YOU.* When you are driving down the highway and you come to a bend in the road, and there is a big yellow sign that says, "Dangerous Curve, Slow Down," the highway department authorities are not trying to scare you, they are trying to save your life by keeping you from going over the edge and by warning you to slow down before you hurt or kill yourself.

When God tells us to: "Enter ye in at the strait gate for wide is the gate, and broad is the way, that leadeth to destruction,... because strait is the gate, and narrow is the way, which leadeth unto life (Matt. 7:13-14), He is not trying to scare you. He is warning you. Hell does not bother me. God can have fourteen different hells in fourteen different locations — hell doesn't bother me in the least, because I don't plan to go there. And if it bothers you, all you have to do is to make sure you are saved and then you will not have to be concerned about hell anymore.

There are many churches where the pastor is not even born again. In some of these churches, in order to meet the requirements for pastoral assignment, all one has to do is to complete four years of undergraduate work, do another three years in graduate school, get a degree in theology, join the denomination, apply for ministerial credentials, answer all the right questions, and the particular denomination will ordain such a candidate as one of theirs. When a parish or church becomes available, the individual can then go and preach at that church, and if the pulpit committee likes him and votes him in, he becomes the pastor of the church, and he may not *even be born again!* This happens all the time. Tragically, it sometimes becomes almost like a game.

Personally I do not have time for playing games. My life is too valuable for that. I love me too much. If you do not understand what I am saying, you may think I am being egotistical. But I am not; I am doing exactly what the Bible told me to do. The Bible told me to love me. If I don't love me, then I have no capacity to love you. The Bible says to love your neighbor as yourself. How can I love you as my neighbor if I do not first of all love myself? That is why some people have problems loving other people, because they do not really love themselves.

If God had wanted you just to love your neighbor, He would have said, "Love your neighbor," period. But isn't it interesting that He said, "Love thy neighbor as thyself" (Matt. 19:19)? In other words, as you love you, love me. There is no way you can love me if you do not love you.

I heard one minister's testimony with my own ears. Here was a man who had a celebrated ministry, a large congregation, was on the radio for thirty-some odd years, was supposedly a minister of the gospel for fifty-two years, and out of his own mouth, he declared that he had never actually been born again. For fifty-two years, he was not even saved. What in the world could he have been preaching all those years? He had to have been preaching nothing much — zero. And the people who listened to him, guess what they got? They got nothing — zero! He had been to college and had several degrees. That is all you need in man's world. *But you need to be born again if you are going to preach in God's world.* Unless you have been born again, you cannot even understand the Bible. That is why there is so much confusion. So many ministers who are in leadership positions have not even been saved.

As I said before, God is not confused. If another pastor and myself are teaching the same thing and he is filled with the Holy Ghost, and I am filled with the Holy Ghost, the Holy Ghost is not going to give him one direction and then turn around and give me another direction about the same thing. No! If we are operating by the same Spirit, we are going to both go in the same direction. When we have one preacher saying, "It is this way," and another saying, "No, it's this way." *THAT CANNOT BE GOD!*

GOD'S WORDS ARE SPIRIT AND LIFE!

God uses the same physical configuration of words as we do, but the meaning behind the words is spiritual. If you do not understand the spirit behind the words, then you will misinterpret and misunderstand what God is talking about. The words of God are only addressed to people who have new spirits — new spirits from God that are calibrated to receive from the same wave length that God is using to beam His messages. For example, there is no point in someone getting upset with the television set and beating on it with a sledgehammer because he wants to see what is playing on Channel 2 when he is tuned into Channel 45. Channel 2 is on VHF and he is on UHF. You have to be on VHF to pick up VHF, and you have to be on UHF to pickup UHF. You have to have a radio receiver that is calibrated to FM to pick up FM transmissions and AM to pick up an AM transmission.

God has a transmission, but if you are not on the same wave length as He is, even though He is beaming His signal out all the time, you are not going to pick it up. The only way you can pick up God's transmission is when you have your receiver fixed and tuned into Him. YOU NEED A NEW RECEIVER. *YOU HAVE TO BE BORN AGAIN, AND THAT GIVES YOU A NEW RECEIVER!*

The Apostle Paul says:

> **But the natural man receiveth not...**
> **(1 Cor. 2:14)**

"The natural man receiveth not...," what does that mean? What is a natural man? *A natural man is a man who has not been BORN AGAIN!* A natural man is a man who has not accepted Christ as his personal Savior. Consequently, all that he can understand are natural things. The spirit-man, on the other hand, has been BORN AGAIN by the Spirit of God, and he *HAS* the capacity to understand spiritual things.

> **But the natural man receiveth not the things of**
> **the Spirit of God: for they are foolishness unto him:**

neither can he know them, because they are spiritually discerned.

(1 Cor. 2:14)

"Discerned" means "understood." *The things of God are spiritually understood.* If a man has not been born again, how can he understand the words of God? He can't — he is at a disadvantage. He can read the Bible all day long, and he still will have no understanding of how to operate in the Word of God.

The people who claim you will be born again when Jesus comes back are trying to put themselves under the Old Covenant. What they are really attempting to do without realizing it is to become righteous in the sight of God through their own merits by trying to keep the Law. When they come to the end of life, they are going to say, "Hey, God, you have to let me in. After all, I went to church every Sabbath day. Saint Peter, open the gate, you have to let me in. I kept the Ten Commandments!" They have not accepted the fact that the only way one can be declared righteous in the sight of God is through the Lord Jesus Christ!

> **Knowing that a man is not justified** [declared righteous] **by the works of the law, but by the faith of Jesus Christ, even we have believed in Jesus Christ, that we might be justified** [or declared righteous] **by the faith of Christ, and not by the works of the law: for by the works of the law shall no flesh be justified.**
> **(Gal. 2:16)**

What does the word *"knowing"* imply? It means you are not *"hoping"* something and you are not *"thinking"* something. When someone says they *"know,"* that means what they know is a foregone conclusion — an established fact. However, when someone says, *"I think,"* or *"I suppose,"* then you know that person is in doubt and whatever he is getting ready to say is not an established fact.

When Paul says *"knowing,"* he is implying that what he is getting ready to say is *revealed truth* and those to whom he is writing ought to know this.

"RIGHTEOUSNESS" MEANS "RIGHT-STANDING WITH GOD"!

Righteousness gives us the ability to enter into the presence of Almighty God, the Creator and Sustainer of the universe, without any sense of feeling "I don't belong here," without any sense of feeling, "I'm not worthy." Rather, he enters into God's presence in righteousness and right-standing because God has granted him this privilege. Too many people do not understand this, and, consequently, they are afraid of God. The Bible says (in Proverbs 1:7): "The fear of the Lord is the beginning of knowledge." That "fear" is not the kind of fear Satan brings, which causes you to be fretful and fearful and full of anxiety. The word "fear," when used concerning God, means "respect and reverence." "The *reverence* of God is the beginning of knowledge (wisdom)." The heavenly Father does not want you to be afraid of Him anymore than any loving parent wants his children to be scared of him.

FRETFULNESS, ANXIETY OR FEAR COMES FROM IGNORANCE OF GOD!

That is what opens the door for Satan to be able to bring the fear in the first place because there is a lack of knowledge about spiritual matters — it is the unfamiliarity of the unknown that brings fear.

The Bible tells us to *"come boldly unto the throne of grace!"* (Heb. 4:16). THANK GOD, WE CAN COME INTO HIS PRESENCE WITHOUT ANY SENSE OF INFERIORITY AND CAN EXPERIENCE FIRST-HAND THE CARE OF THE HEAVENLY FATHER THROUGH OUR LORD JESUS CHRIST!

NO ONE CAN BE JUSTIFIED BY OBEYING THE LAW!

It is absolutely astounding how anyone could read Galatians 2:16 and get hung up on trying to keep the Law — trying to become justified or pleasing to God when it specifically states that *no flesh shall be justified (or declared righteous) by the works of the law!*

It is by the faith of Jesus Christ. You cannot get away from Jesus! You have to enter into the Kingdom by God's way. Many people are trying to do it their way. They are making their own rules and saying that God ought to be pleased with them. "After all, I went to church once last year. God ought to be happy with that. I gave a dollar in the offering. What more does God want me to do?" I tell you what God wants you to do. *He wants you to follow His Word! He wants you to love and respect Him!* "Oh, yes, Brother Price, I love the Lord!" But you wouldn't tithe 10% to God to save your life!

To show you the inconsistency of man, some people will balk at giving God 10 percent, even though He has said that He would open the windows of heaven and pour out a blessing to the tither that there would not be enough room to receive it all. Yet, the same people wouldn't dare walk out of a restaurant without leaving a 15 percent tip for the waiter or waitress, because they do not want anyone to think that they are cheapskates, as though that restaurant or waiter or waitress is supplying their life-line.

"...BY THE WORKS OF THE LAW SHALL NO FLESH BE JUSTIFIED!"

In Romans 7, we see a beautiful revelation concerning this principle:

> **Know ye not, brethren, (for I speak to them that know the law,)...** [It is obvious, then, that Paul is addressing himself to Jews. He would not be addressing himself to Gentiles, because Gentiles, as such, did not know the Law.] **Know ye not, brethren, (for I speak to them that know the law,) how that the law hath dominion over a man as long as he liveth? For the woman which hath an husband is bound by the law to her husband as long as he liveth; but if the husband be dead, she is loosed from the law of her husband. So then if, while her husband liveth, she be married to another man, she shall be called an adulteress: but if her husband be dead, she is free from that law; so that she is no adulteress, though she be married to another man. Wherefore, my brethren, ye also are become dead to the law by the body of Christ; that ye should be married to another, even to him who is raised from the dead, that we should bring forth fruit unto God.**
>
> (Rom. 7:1-4)

As I was preparing for this study, I was directed to this particular passage and I saw something that I had never seen before. When I previously read that passage of Scripture, I always thought Paul was talking about husbands and wives. I always thought he was talking about divorce and was trying to show us what not to do and what to do concerning divorce. But as I really began to delve into this particular subject about the Law, I discovered that Paul is not talking about husbands and wives here at all. He is not talking about divorce at all. He is talking about whether or not the Church is under the Mosaic Law, and he is simply using husbands and wives as a parable.

Paul is talking to the Jews, because the Jews were the only ones who were ever under the Law. He is showing the Jews that when Jesus died on the cross, every Jew died in Jesus to the Law.

According to the Bible, the heavenly Father identifies us with Christ. I died in Christ, I was buried with Christ, I rose with Christ, I ascended with Christ and I am seated together with Christ in heavenly places. What Paul is saying to the Jew is that when Jesus rose from the dead, *the Law was fulfilled and set aside.*

When Jesus walked the earth and taught among the Jews, they accused him of breaking the Law. He told them He had come to "fulfill the law and the prophets." This means, then, that *JESUS IS THE FULFILLMENT OF THE LAW!* Everything in the Law pointed to Jesus. He is the fulfillment of the Law which includes the Law of the Sabbath, the Ten Commandments and the Law of Moses. When something is fulfilled, guess what? It means it is over, finished and done with.

When Jesus rose from the dead, the Law was fulfilled and set aside. Now, the Jew could marry Jesus and not be considered to be an adulteress. Remember,

Paul said that the Law was effective as long as the woman's husband was alive, and if she were to marry another man while her husband was alive, she would be considered an adulteress. However, if her husband died, she was free from that law and she could marry again and would not be considered an adulteress.

Here is the punch line! *If a man were keeping the Law and still trying to be married to Jesus, HE WAS AN ADULTERER!* He could not be married to Christ and keep the Law — he would have two wives, and the Bible calls that adultery!

In Galatians 4, it is interesting to note that Paul says the very same thing, but he is saying it in a different way. When you read the letter to the Galatians, the word "Galatians" is pluralized. This letter was written to a certain geographical area during the time in which Paul lived. In that particular area there were many churches, and this letter was sent out and circulated among these churches. There had been several churches which had been telling the Gentiles that they had to keep the Law of Moses in order to be saved. Paul wrote the letter to the churches of Galatia in order to correct this fallacy because people were being held in bondage. Just like churches today have people in bondage by trying to have them follow the Law and the Ten Commandments, while at the same time trying to walk with Jesus. You cannot do both! *IT IS SPIRITUAL ADULTERY,* and you grieve the Spirit of God when you try to combine both these entities.

My little children, of whom I travail in birth again until Christ be formed in you, I desire to be

present with you now, and to change my voice; for I stand in doubt of you. Tell me, ye that desire to be under the law, do ye not hear the law? For it is written, that Abraham had two sons. [Let us stop right here before proceeding. In order to get the picture of what is being said here, we need to do a little interpreting and to substitute some things so that we will be able to follow along to see the point Paul is trying to make. Paul says that Abraham had two sons. Think of the two sons as one of them being the Law of Moses (the Old Covenant), and the other son as being the "New Creation" (the New Covenant).] **For it is written, that Abraham had two sons, the one by a bondmaid, the other by a freewoman. But he who was of the bond-woman was born after the flesh; but he of the freewoman was by promise. Which things are an allegory** [picture story]: **for these are the two covenants; the one from the mount Sinai, which gendereth to bondage, which is Agar** [or actually Hagar]. [Abraham was well stricken in years and he and his wife, Sara, had had no children. Like any good, red-blooded man, Abraham wanted to have a son to carry on his posterity. God came to Abraham and made a promise to him that he would have a son after a certain period of time; however, Abraham and Sara became impatient. God was too slow for them, so they tried to help Him out. Sara had her maid, Hagar, conceive for her by Abraham. This was an acceptable practice during that time. The child to be born would be considered Sara's. That was strictly after the flesh. Abraham and Sara allowed their flesh to get in the way, but, praise God, it did not stop God's promise to them from being fulfilled. (Gen. 16:1-5) This is what being talked about in verse 24.] **Which things are an allegory: for these are the two covenants; the one from the mount Sinai, which gendereth to bondage, which is Agar.** [That is exactly what the Law did — it put people in bondage, and that is exactly what it is doing now!] **For this Agar is mount**

Sinai in Arabia, and answereth to Jerusalem which now is, and is in bondage with her children. [Paul is talking about two covenants — Isaac and Ishmael or Sara and Hagar. Hagar represents the Old Covenant, which has to do with the flesh. The boy-child, Ishmael, came as the result of the action of the flesh, not by the promise of God. Isaac, on the other hand, was the product of the promise that God made representing the New Covenant. Now drop down to verse 28.] **Now we, brethren, as Isaac was, are the children of promise.** [Notice how Paul relates it to Isaac — the child of promise. He says that we who are in Christ are the heirs of the New Covenant by promise.] **But as then he that was born after the flesh persecuted him that was born after the Spirit, even so is it now.** These folks who try to keep the Law will persecute those of us who don't. They will call you everything but a child of God; they will try to put the screws to you, tighten down on you, and tell you that you are not a Christian if you do not go to church on Saturday or if you do not keep the Ten Commandments.] **Nevertheless what saith the scripture? Cast out the bondwoman and her son: for the son of the bondwoman shall not be heir with the son of the freewoman. So then, brethren, we are not children of the bondwoman, but of the free.**

(Gal. 4:19-31)

Paul said this was an allegory or a parable or a story. He used Abraham, Sara and Hagar, along with Ishmael and Isaac, to compare the Old Covenant with the New.

If the bondwoman and her son represent the Old Covenant (the Law of Moses, and all that went with the Law), if we are to be true to the allegory, when it says, ''cast out the bondwoman and her son,'' so that the son of promise, Isaac (the New Covenant), can operate, then that means that we, as New Covenant

Believers, are to cast out the Law and cast out the Ten Commandments because they represent Hagar, which is the flesh, and the promise was not made to the flesh, so get rid of it.

Can you see that? That means we are not under the Law. There is no way in the world God could want us under the Law because we are the seed of Isaac by promise.

Some people will get a little upset about this, because they think that what I am saying is that Christians have no law! *WE DO HAVE A LAW — WE DO HAVE A COMMANDMENT!*

We are not lawless; we have a law, we have a covenant and we have a commandment in that covenant which Jesus gave us. As I covered in previous sections of this book, our law, commandment and covenant are found in the thirteenth chapter of John, verses 34-35. *IT IS THE COMMANDMENT, LAW AND COVENANT OF LOVE!*

Let us review some more Scripture concerning the Law being done away with.

> **Is the law then against the promises of God? God forbid....** [In other words, no, it is not. The Law was there to fulfill the promises of God, and the end of the Law is the fulfillment of the promise of God.] **Is the law then against the promises of God? God forbid: for if there had been a law given which could have given life....** [That ought to tell us, then, that the Law must have to do with death and not life, because if the Law had to do only with life, Paul wouldn't then say, "for if there had been a law given which could have given life" — the opposite of life is death. Jesus said

that He came to bring us life more abundantly. He did not come to bring death, but He came to bring life!]

(Gal. 3:21)

Let's look at the rest of this passage from Galatians:

Is the law then against the promises of God? God forbid: for if there had been a law given which could have given life, verily RIGHTEOUSNESS SHOULD HAVE BEEN BY THE LAW. [But since there wasn't any law that could give life, then that means righteousness cannot come by the Law.] **But the scripture hath concluded all under sin, that the promise by faith of Jesus Christ might be given to them that believe.** [Not to them that follow the Law, but to them that believe. This is talking about those of us who have accepted Christ as our personal Savior. That is the reason why Jesus is so important. Some folks get all upset when you talk about Jesus. Many of them think, "Well, I'm just as good as those Christians. I don't have to go to church; I'm just as educated and just as intelligent as anyone else and I don't need any church telling me what to do. I am a morally good person: I don't rob banks, I don't commit murder, I don't commit rape, I don't cheat on my income tax, I don't, I don't, and so on." These people are on their way to hell! You do not score any goodie points with God just because you think you are moral. It is not what you think anyway; IT'S WHAT GOD THINKS THAT COUNTS.]

Notice what Paul says in Galatians 3:22:

But the scripture hath concluded all under sin, that the promise by faith of Jesus Christ might be given to them that believe.

The Law could not or cannot give righteousness or eternal life — only the finished work of Jesus Christ can do that — only through Christ can anyone have life.

> **But before faith came, we were kept under the law...**
>
> **(Gal. 3:23)**

One of the things we have to do when we read the Bible is to learn how to *rightly* divide what we read. Second Timothy 2:15 says: "Study to shew thyself approved unto God, a workman that needeth not to be ashamed, *rightly dividing the word of truth.*"

The reason it says "rightly dividing" is because it is possible to "wrongly divide" — if you do not study. If there were no danger of wrongly dividing, there would not be any need to say "rightly."

In verse 23, we have to use the principle of rightly dividing. Normally in the New Testament books when it says "us," "we" and "ours," it is referring to the Body of Christ. However, sometimes these pronouns are referring to the nation of Israel. The context of what is being said helps us to know who is being addressed. Paul says, "But before faith came, we were kept under the law," and he is talking about the Jews, not the Gentiles.

You might ask, "Well, how do you know that?" The next clause lets us know: "But before faith came, *we were kept under the law*" (Gal. 3:23). You could not have been kept under the Law as a Gentile, because the Law was never given to Gentiles or to Christians.

This letter, of course, was written to the Jewish saints in Galatia to set them free from bondage to the

Law. Some Jewish Christians were telling other Jewish Christians that they had to keep the Law in order to be saved, and Paul wrote this epistle (or letter) to correct this error. Notice again:

> **But before faith came, we were kept under the law, shut up unto the faith which should afterwards be revealed.**
>
> **(Gal. 3:23)**

HERE IS ANOTHER REVELATION!

The word "afterwards" implies something was before, but "afterwards," by virtue of its designation, indicates that the thing it came after is not in operation anymore. It is the time "afterwards" that counts. What is the "afterwards" — IT IS AFTER THE LAW! What is implied here is that the Law is outdated, dead.

That's why the "afterwards" is operating.

> **Wherefore the law was our schoolmaster to bring us unto Christ, that we might be justified by faith.**
>
> **(Gal. 3:24)**

The word *"was"* is a past-tense designation, indicating that the time of the action has already taken place. Notice it does not say, "the law is (present tense)," it doesn't say, "the law will be (future tense);" it says "the law *WAS!*" Whatever "was," isn't anymore. Because if it were, it would not be "was.")

> **But after that faith is come, we are no longer under a schoolmaster.**
>
> **(Gal. 3:25)**

You have to be deaf, dumb, blind or dishonest not to see that! That is as clear as it can be.

The schoolmaster in those days was a person who went through the community ringing a little bell, alerting all the students that it was time for school, and all the children would come out of their homes and follow the schoolmaster to the schoolhouse or wherever they were having their assembly. When the children got into the classroom, that was the end of the job of the schoolmaster. His job simply was to lead the children from where they were to where they should be in order to receive instruction.

That is the analogy Paul is using. Now with that analogy in mind, let's cover verses 24-25 again:

> **Wherefore the law was our schoolmaster to bring us unto Christ, that we might be justified by faith** [NOT BY THE LAW]. [It is obvious that the Law was the schoolmaster to bring us to Christ, and it is just as obvious that once you get to Christ, you do not need the schoolmaster anymore.] **But after that faith is come, we are no longer under a schoolmaster.**
> **(Gal. 3:24-25)**

Paul said that the Law was our schoolmaster to bring us to Christ. Now that we are in Christ, where faith has brought us, we do not need the schoolmaster any longer.

Since the schoolmaster represents the Law, if we don't need the schoolmaster, we don't need the Law. If we don't need the Law, *WE ARE NOT UNDER IT. THEREFORE, WE DO NOT HAVE TO KEEP IT!*

According to the Scriptures we have studied, I believe the Bible clearly teaches that *every man, woman, boy, or girl who is attempting to keep the Law (unless he or she has been born again previously) IS NOT BORN AGAIN!* And he or she is in perilous circumstances — he or she is hellbound.

Most people don't like to talk about hell, but that is tough! That is just the way it is. Hell is there — the Bible says so! I didn't invent it, I didn't create it and I don't plan to go there. However, I would be derelict in my duties as a Christian and as a minister of the gospel if I did not tell people about it.

YOU DO NOT HAVE TO GO TO HELL!

You don't have to argue about it, or fuss about it, or get into any philosophical deliberations as to whether there is or there isn't a hell. *The Bible says there is*, and what anyone else says is irrelevant and immaterial.

There are many people following certain denominations or what we might call cults. This is sad, because these people are headed for a Christless eternity. What is truly tragic is that most of these people are sincere, and yet they are sincerely wrong. They are not wrong because I say they are wrong, they are wrong because they are not in line with God's Word.

Understand that those people, who had already accepted Christ at some point in their lives but later got sucked into one of the religious groups that teach the law of the Sabbath and the Ten Commandments are still saved; however, they are being cheated and robbed out of what they ought to have in this life under their New Covenant rights, and that, too, is tragic.

The Bible says in the mouth of two or three witnesses, let every word be established (Matt. 18:16). Therefore, I want to cover four more Scriptures that will show us clearly that trying to keep the Law will not work.

> **But that no man is justified** [or declared righteous] **by the law in the sight of God, it is evident: for, The just** [or those who have been declared righteous] **shall live by faith.**
>
> **(Gal. 3:11)**

Notice the importance of the words, *"in the sight of God."* You may be justified in the sight of your church, you may be justified in the sight of the preacher, you may be justified in the sight of the bishop or Pope or whoever, *but you are not justified in the SIGHT OF GOD!*

Friend, the bottom line is to please the heavenly Father. When you come before the Judge of all the ages, it is what He thinks about you that counts.

> **Therefore by the deeds of the law there shall no flesh be justified** [declared righteous] **in his sight: for by the law is the knowledge of sin.**
>
> **(Rom. 3:20)**

> **For by grace are ye saved through faith; and that not of yourselves: it is the gift of God.**
>
> **(Eph. 2:8)**

We are saved not by keeping the Law, not by going to church on Saturdays, not by observing the Ten Commandments — but by faith!

Stand fast therefore in the liberty wherewith Christ hath made us free, and be not entangled again with the yoke of bondage.

(Gal. 5:1)

Here Paul is telling the Jewish converts to stand fast in the liberty of the New Covenant.

The Israelites were the servants of Jehovah, but we, as Christians, have been given the privilege through Jesus Christ to be called the children of God, whereby we can cry, "Abba, Father."

So, stand fast in the liberty that has been given to you under the New Covenant and not be entangled again with the yoke of bondage, which is the Old Covenant — the Law!

For a complete list of tapes and books by Fred Price,
or to receive his publication, *Ever Increasing Faith
Messenger*, write:

Fred Price
Crenshaw Christian Center
P. O. Box 90000
Los Angeles, CA 90009

Books by Frederick K.C. Price, Ph.D.

HIGH FINANCE
(God's Financial Plan: Tithes and Offerings)

HOW FAITH WORKS
(In English and Spanish)

IS HEALING FOR ALL?

HOW TO OBTAIN STRONG FAITH
(Six Principles)

NOW FAITH IS

THE HOLY SPIRIT —
The Missing Ingredient

FAITH, FOOLISHNESS, OR PRESUMPTION?

THANK GOD FOR EVERYTHING?

HOW TO BELIEVE GOD FOR A MATE

MARRIAGE AND THE FAMILY
Practical Insight for Family Living

LIVING IN THE REALM OF THE SPIRIT

THE ORIGIN OF SATAN

CONCERNING THEM WHICH ARE ASLEEP

HOMOSEXUALITY:
State of Birth or State of Mind?

PROSPERITY ON GOD'S TERMS

WALKING IN GOD'S WORD
(Through His Promises)

KEYS TO SUCCESSFUL MINISTRY

NAME IT AND CLAIM IT!
The Power of Positive Confession

THE VICTORIOUS, OVERCOMING LIFE
(A Verse-by-Verse Study of the Book of Colossians)

A NEW LAW FOR A NEW PEOPLE

THE FAITHFULNESS OF GOD

THE PROMISED LAND
(A New Era for the Body of Christ)

Available from your local bookstore

Frederick K.C. Price, Ph.D., founded Crenshaw Christian Center in Los Angeles, California in 1973 with a congregation of some 300 people. Today, the church membership numbers well over 14,000 people of various racial backgrounds.

Crenshaw Christian Center, home of the renowned 10,140-seat FaithDome, has a staff of more than 200 employees. CCC consists of a Ministry Training Institute, which includes a School of Ministry, School of the Bible, and a Helps Ministry Summer School. There is also the Frederick K.C. Price, III Elementary, and Junior and Senior High Schools, as well as a Child Care Center.

"EVER INCREASING FAITH" Television and Radio broadcasts are outreaches of Crenshaw Christian Center. The television program is viewed on more than 100 stations throughout the United States and overseas. The radio program airs on approximately 50 stations across the country.

Dr. Price travels extensively teaching the WORD OF FAITH simply and understandably in the power of the Holy Spirit. He is the author of several books on faith and divine healing.

In 1990, Dr. Price founded the "FELLOWSHIP OF INNER-CITY WORD OF FAITH MINISTRIES (FICWFM)" for the purpose of fostering and spreading the faith message among independent ministries located in the urban, metropolitan areas of the United States.